Cities Without Cities

Cities Without Cities investigates the social, economic, environmental and formal/structural characteristics of today's built environment: no longer simply a city but increasingly large conurbations made up of a number of development clusters, linked by transport routes. The diffusion of the once compact city into city web, the *Zwischenstadt* is mirrored by changes in society from communities with strong social cohesion and social links, with little interest in their own town or city other than the quality of their personal space.

The account is complex and on a number of levels: social philosophical, economic and environmental. The difficulties in managing or even controlling the city web, divided arbitrarily into areas of limited size and political power, are enormous. Areas compete with each other rather than cooperate. The book provides a better understanding of this new type of urban form and argues for a change in planning systems for better management.

The book formulates a fundamental critique of the ideal of the compact city as not feasible any more, but it also sketches an optimistic outlook on the challenge of planning and designing the urban landscape.

Thomas Sieverts is Emeritus Professor at the University of Darmstadt and he has written this book as Fellow of the Institute of Advanced Studies in Berlin. He has also previously lectured in planning and urban design in both the UK and the USA. He is partner of SKAT Architects Town Planners in Bonn, and an advisor to the German government.

Other titles available from Spon Press

Towards an Urban Renaissance
The Urban Task Force

Urban Future 21
A Global Agenda for Twenty-First Century Cities
Peter Hall and Ulrich Pfeiffer

The Chosen City
Nicholas Schoon

Global City Regions
Their Emerging Forms
Roger Simmonds and Gary Hack

Cities for the New Millennium
Marcial Echenique and Andrew Saint

For further information and to order from our online catalogue visit our website at www.sponpress.com

Cities Without Cities

An interpretation of the
Zwischenstadt

Thomas Sieverts

Spon Press
Taylor & Francis Group

LONDON AND NEW YORK

Published 2003 by Spon Press
11 New Fetter Lane, London EC4P 4EE

Simultaneously published in the USA and Canada
by Routledge
29 West 35th Street, New York, NY 10001

Spon Press is an imprint of the Taylor & Francis Group

English language edition 2003 © 2003 Spon Press

First published 1997 by Vieweg
Reprinted 1998 (twice), 1999

Reprinted 2001 by Birkhäuser

Original German language edition Zwischenstadt, © 2000, Birkhäuser,
Switzerland.

Translated by Daniel de Lough

Typeset in Sabon by Wearset Ltd, Boldon, Tyne and Wear
Printed and bound in Great Britain by TJ International Ltd, Padstow,
Cornwall

The publication of this book was sponsored by funds from the Goethe
Institut Inter Nationes, Bonn

Cover image: Our Towns and Cities: The Future Delivering and Urban
Renaissance. Cm 4911.
Crown copyright is reproduced with the permission of the Controller
of Her Majesty's Stationery Office and the Queen's Printer for
Scotland.

British Library Cataloguing in Publication Data
A catalogue record for this book is available from the British Library

Library of Congress Cataloging in Publication Data
Sieverts, Thomas.
 [Zwischenstadt. English]
 Cities without cities : an interpretation of the Zwischenstadt /
Thomas Sieverts.–English language ed.
  p. cm.
 Includes bibliographical references and index.
 1. Urbanization–Germany. 2. Regional planning–Germany. I Title.
 HT384.G3 S54 2003
 307.76'0943–dc22

ISBN 0-415-27259-9 hb
ISBN 0-415-27260-2 pb

Contents

Foreword to the English edition

'*Zwischenstadt*', the German title of this book, has become a common term in the public discussion of urban form and structure in German-speaking countries. The title is difficult to translate. Therefore, it might be helpful for the English-speaking reader to link the book to the Anglo-Saxon discussion of urban affairs. Essentially, the book deals with the discrepancy between urban reality and prevailing ideologies of what a European city should be. It calls upon the reader to take reality seriously and be careful with criticisms rooted in an ideological concept of the city.

In Britain, the discrepancy between new realities and old theoretical concepts is quite old. In 1902, more than a hundred years ago, H. G. Wells predicted the emergence of a new type of city in the second chapter, 'The Probable Diffusion of Cities', of his book *Anticipations*. His prediction meets our present reality in an astonishing way: 'these coming cities will not be, in the old sense, cities at all; they will present a new and entirely different phase of human distribution'.[1] Towards the end of the chapter he predicts:

> the city will diffuse itself until it has taken up considerable areas and many of the characteristics, the greenness, the fresh air, of what is now country, [and this] leads us to suppose also that the country will take to itself many of the qualities of the city. The old antithesis will indeed cease, the boundary lines will altogether disappear; it will become, indeed, merely a question of more or less populous. There will be horticulture and agriculture going on within the 'urban regions', and 'urbanity' without them. Everywhere, indeed, over the land of the globe between the frozen circles, the railway and the new

roads will spread, the network of communication wires and safe and convenient ways. To receive the daily paper a few hours late, to wait a day or so for goods one has ordered, will be the extreme measure of rusticity safe in a few remote islands and inaccessible places. The character of the meshes in that wider network of roads that will be the country, as distinguished from the urban district, will vary with the soil, the climate and the tenure of the land – will vary too with the racial and national differences. But throughout all that follows, this mere relativity of the new sort of town to the new sort of country over which the new sorts of people ... will be scattered, must be borne in mind.[2]

Wells described more or less precisely the reality of our contemporary large cities and agglomerations as a continuum of built-up areas and open space, connected by a network of paths of different size and character. As an eminent intellectual, he accepted this coming reality as an appropriate form of settlement for the new society.

Only a few years earlier, in 1898, Ebenezer Howard had developed in his book *Tomorrow: A Peaceful Path to Real Reform* a theoretical, diagrammatic conception of how to deal with the seemingly boundless growth and expansion of the metropolis. He tried to reformulate the concept of the urban entity of the European city in contrast to, and with defined boundaries towards, the countryside. Howard's book inspired a strong trend that still influences the thinking of urban planners all over the world. In the UK, for example, it led to the New Town Policy of post-1947 governments. This policy aimed to prevent the further growth of London and the cities in the Midlands and Scotland and, by doing so, to secure the traditional open countryside.

However, this aim was not so successfully accomplished. Despite the New Towns, the cities grew in the way H. G. Wells had predicted. Even the commendable report of the Urban Task Force *Towards an Urban Renaissance* in 1999 basically still follows the tradition of Ebenezer Howard by promoting the compact urban entity with a hierarchical order of functions and services. The government White Paper *Our Towns and Cities*[3] will hopefully lead to the restructuring of our run-down cities. However, the other reality of our town–country continuum described by H. G. Wells will continue to exist and grow: the 'urbanised landscape' or 'landscaped city'.

This book *Cities Without Cities* tries to increase awareness of this strange urban–rural landscape as a new form of city. In attempting to do this, it discusses issues such as: the increasingly fractured form of the boundaries between urban fabric and open space and nature; the gradual disappearance of the traditional hierarchical pattern; and the mutual penetration of built forms and landscapes.

No doubt, this urban landscape has American features. The socio-economic forces which H. G. Wells describes in his astonishing book have been able to develop in the United States with fewer restrictions than in Europe. But even in the United States the influence of Ebenezer Howard is obvious, from Clarence Stein's New Towns, in President Roosevelt's 'New Deal' to the recent movement of 'The New Urbanism' with its aim to create the structure and image of the old American country town as a critical response to urban sprawl. Since President Jefferson's time, the United States has never had as strict a distinction as Europe between the compact town and open country. Its conurbations contain an almost unlimited urbanised landscape for which Frank Lloyd Wright developed the notion of 'Broadacre City' as an essentially American concept. For the American reader, it might be interesting to note that in Europe there are growing concerns to preserve and create typical European characteristics not only for the city proper but also in the urbanised landscape or landscaped city. This urban landscape might have the following features:

- the creation of 'regional parks', including agriculture, which give the remaining open space a distinct form and complex function and make them resistant to further sprawl;
- the maintenance or establishment of threshold population densities in the corridors of the built-up areas, viably served by public transport; and
- the preservation or creation of public nodes of centrality as focal points even though they are not hierarchical in their functions.

It is very important that the nodes and settlements are connected by a continuous network of transportation routes and paths of different types and capacities. Hopefully, the European character will also lead to a new aesthetics, transforming the 'deserts of non-aesthetics' of today into realms people care about. Such a strategy, combining old European tradition with new reality, would have pleased, so we believe, even H. G. Wells.

A note on the term *Zwischenstadt*

The term *Zwischenstadt* signifies that today's city is in an 'in between' state, a state between place and world, space and time, city and country. Considerable efforts were made to find an appropriate English translation for the main title, and proposals ranged from 'intermediate city' to 'meta city', the latter having been used in other English publications on the forming of urban regions. Yet, the meaning of none of the English terms investigated is quite the same as that of *Zwischenstadt* in which – as the author summarises at the end of the book – place-specific actions of nation-states, cities and communities are strongly influenced by international actions and the global market, in which the speed of information and travel connections has blurred the notion of space, in which the old contrast between city and country has dissolved into a city–country continuum.

Authors, publisher and translators agreed in the end to do what is also considered for the French translation of this book: to keep the original German term in the text, but to add this note which should help the reader understand its meaning and significance. As the text addresses both the notion of the city cluster *per se* and the occurrence of many of such clusters throughout the world, we provide a technical note: *Zwischenstadt* is the singular, *Zwischenstädte* is the plural form of the term.

Thomas Sieverts and Hildebrand Frey
Glasgow, December 2002

Notes

1 Wells, H. G. (1902) *Anticipations of the Reaction of Mechanical and Scientific Progress upon Human Life and Thought*, eighth edition, Chapman & Hall, London, p. 40.
2 Ibid., pp. 63–64.
3 Department of the Environment, Transport and the Regions (2000) *Our Towns and Cities: The Future – Delivering an Urban Renaissance*, HMSO, London.

Foreword

This book deals with the dissolution of the compact historical European city and with the treatment of a completely different and new form of the city, which is spreading across the world: the urbanised landscape or the landscaped city. For the sake of simplicity I call this *Zwischenstadt*, meaning the type of built-up area that is between the old historical city centres and the open countryside, between the place as a living space and the non-places of movement, between small local economic cycles and the dependency on the world market.

In order to avoid one misunderstanding in advance, let me make it clear that this book is not a plea in favour of dispersed settlement, of urban sprawl. I am just as keen on the form and nature of the historical European city and the historical cultural landscape as my colleagues who still today heroically try to defend it as a model for the future against all the devilish forces of dissolution. Who would not be pleased if cities could be kept compact, villages intact and the natural landscape unscathed? Perhaps it is even justified to continue to call for the old conventions and objectives in the hope that at least something of them remains valid, although the reality is getting further and further away from these ideals. By calling into question the validity of conventions which the guild of planners has adopted as its broadly agreed principles of planning – such as the principle of 'decentralised concentration', of 'regulating intervention and compensation', of 'land saving through high building densities', or even the ordering system of 'centralised locations' and 'small grain mixed use' – we find ourselves occupying an uncomfortable position between all camps. The idealists among the planners accuse the critics of a betrayal of sublime principles – and that is painful; investors and technocrats of all types could use the criticism to justify their limited actions – and that would be dangerous; and the politicians could then feel themselves challenged to pay still less attention to spatial planning than they have done so far, instead of seeing the major new political design opportunities which the *Zwischenstadt* offers – and that would be disastrous!

The dilemma seems unavoidable, because the 'Golden Age', of an enlightened, well-funded and well-equipped European system of public intervention with a 'golden rein' – where town planning, despite much uneasiness, could feel at home and where a ceasefire, if not exactly a peace, prevailed between municipal corporations and capital – is over. Sometimes, among my guild of architects and urban designers, I feel like a guild master at the beginning of the nineteenth century, previously able to maintain the old rules and practices to some extent against mercantilism – although not without losing some of his beautiful, colourful plumage – but who now has to protect himself against the rise of capitalism and so suffers one defeat after another, because he misjudges the forces of the age. Sometimes I have a frustrating feeling that, with our efforts to save the archetype of the historical European city as a model for the future, we urban designers today are only delivering the public fig leaf for developments which run in a quite different direction and in a completely different environment. With an ecological approach, which predominantly concentrates on the symptoms only, not much is going to be achieved. Sometimes I get the impression that our guild has forgotten how to think politic-ally and to draw distinctions between social changes, movements and forces -which we, whether we like it or not, have to recognise as preconditions for planning because we can change hardly any-thing about them – and such developments as we can influence and structure. However, only when we can do that, will we be able to get involved with any prospect of having an effect.

The fundamental changes that we will have to accept as pre-conditions are well known, for example:

1   the worldwide distribution of labour in the economy and the change that this means for the position of the city in the struc-ture of the world economy;
2   the dissolution of the cultural binding forces of the city and

the radical pluralisation of city culture which is connected with it;

3 the fact that the natural world has now been almost completely penetrated by artefacts and the contrast between city and nature has therefore dissolved.

In combination, these changes and forces are leading to a profound transformation of the city which could destroy the European city but which – and this is the core thesis of this book – is also opening up the possibility of new design perspectives. In the context of a globalisation which can no longer be held back, thinking through these changes confronts us with the task of finding and developing, in the course of its transformation, new forms of the European city. In these the historical city is protected and sublimated as a special part of the city if only because, once it is destroyed, it cannot be reconstructed. To be sure, in the interest of maintaining its essential characteristics, the historical core will have to give up specific central tasks and thus become one part of the city among others – albeit of a unique kind. In this way, and by responding to place-specific conditions, Europe could make a unique contribution to achieving a European characterisation of the global city model. Although this would have links with the great traditions of the European city, it would not be in a defensive, retrospectively orientated manner, but in an extensive perception of the immense new possibilities which globalisation offers in addition to all its negative aspects. I am convinced that this task opens up a field for design which is as productive as it is rewarding for politicians and town planners, even though this might seem almost utopian today.

In Europe, town planning and urban design were children of the crises of liberalism in the age of the Industrial Revolution. Initially they arose to repair the worst side effects of city expansion: epidemics of cholera and typhus, outbreaks of fire and desperate living conditions. Modern town planning and urban development as approaches to the taming and cultivation of capitalism only came into effect much later, but even in the early utopian and reforming conceptions they were laid out in perspective. As far as I am concerned, even today urban design still belongs to this tradition of European town planning, as a constant challenge to protect the endangered weaker elements of the city – human beings, nature and culture – and develop them in their own values with their own inherent characteristics. The conditions for efficacy in urban design construed in this way have altered sharply again since the epochal change in world history in 1989, a turning point to a new expansion of global market forces which transcend nation-states and in turn are having highly deleterious ecological and social side-effects. Confronted with this, should we not still continue to believe that society will be able to mobilise counter-forces, to discover new opportunities and to answer the questions which today seem to be put from an almost utopian perspective? Do the debates about communitarianism, about the necessary new reorientation to social well-being – and also the discussions about a new balance of competition and cooperation, of planning and self-regulation, of state and intermediate institutions – not reveal approaches to a new understanding of town planning? These debates are very much in a European tradition. The present book is intended to make a contribution to this debate. It is a plea to perceive the opportunities of the *Zwischenstadt*.

The subject is not a new one; seen in the historical perspective, urban development is usually concerned with recurrent themes in a long tradition of ideas and concepts. With my questions, I connect my subject with a European debate about modernity from immediately after the First World War which, here in Berlin, where this book was written, is connected with Bruno Taut and Hans Scharoun. 'In his work *The Dissolution of Cities*, Taut formulated the prospects of human globalisation in a pacifist euphoria with dreamy visions of bands of settlements covering the world' (Durth).[1] Hans Scharoun's concept of the urban landscape, as, for example, in his plan for Berlin after the Second World War, also falls into this tradition. There are many other examples from the history of ideas of urban development that could be mentioned which, rooted in a criticism of the densely composed city, demand the dissolution of the city. These range from the early socialist Robert Owen with his communes, in which industry and agriculture were to be combined, through Frank Lloyd Wright's archetypal American Broadacre City, in which land ownership forms the basis of social collaboration, up to the half-European half-American Ludwig Hilberseimer with his bands of settlements cutting through the US prairie. However, historical perspectives are not the subject of this book (individual, detailed references can be found in the notes). The emphasis is on the present and on the argument about a restorative conception of the city, which has been predominant for a generation and not only in Berlin. No attempt will be made to base the force of the argument on the history of ideas, and the line of argument will frequently appeal less to seminal texts than to their specialist interpreters. The book should be regarded not as an enlightened analysis without anger and passion but as a polemic and a challenge to action. The five chapters each consider the *Zwischenstadt* from a different perspective. Description, analysis and proposals for action interlock, in order to render the relation to action of the line of thought palpable. This means that questions about images and about the readability of the *Zwischenstadt* are constantly taken up.

The argument presented by this book is structured as follows. The first chapter focuses on the urban environments of the *Zwischenstadt*. A brief description of the urbanised landscape is given and the myth of the Old City is subjected to a critical analysis of five key concepts, the meaning and use of which are at present prominently oriented towards such a myth.

In the second chapter, building up from the basis of this criticism, a new perspective for the urbanised landscape is developed. This perspective is subjected to a political critique with reference to the theoretical stance of Alain Touraine. This determines a political position from which seven theses on the need for the intelligibility and legibility of the *Zwischenstadt* are developed.

In the third chapter, the urbanised landscape as a space for day-to-day life is considered and criticised from the political position that has now been developed. A perspective is drafted for a living space characterised by the principle of a 'cycle economy', in which awareness for sustainability becomes paramount.

The subject of the fourth chapter is a cultural and design-oriented interpretation of the *Zwischenstadt* in its diversity as against the familiar historical city and the importance of cultural policy for its design.

In the fifth and final chapter an attempt is made to sketch a perspective for a new form of regional planning and regional policy.

This book was written in the academic year 1995/96 in the stimulating environment of the Institute for Advanced Studies in Berlin, which I would here like to thank for a unique quality of life. Petra Sonnenberg transferred the various forms of my hand-written manuscript into computer form and read through the corrections with patience and care. Ulrich Conrads, as a reader and friend, prepared the manuscript for printing. Important discussion partners for the work as co-fellows were Susanne Hauser and Michael Mönninger, the latter precisely also with his differences of opinion. Werner Durth, who was to be with me in the Institute but was unfortunately unable to take up the invitation, as a friend of many years, helped me with references to the literature on the history of ideas and with well-grounded criticism; what a pity that we were not able to discuss these matters in the Institute's environment! With Sibylle Ebe I examined the manuscript for intelligibility and applicability to practice and in walks through the *Zwischenstadt* checked it for clarity. Hille von Seggern, with whom I have also had many years of stimulating discussions, contributed to clarifying my ideas with questions on my basic understanding of planning, as also did Ursula Stein. Hanns Adrian should really be mentioned as the co-author of two chapters, provided that he should not as result have to bear responsibility for the remainder of the book. All these friends and colleagues I would like to thank warmly for their constructive criticism. However, without my five years of experience as one of the Directors of the 'Internationale Bauausstellung Emscher Park' (International Building Exhibition Emscher Park) in the Ruhr area, without many thought-provoking discussions with my colleagues there – above all with the animator and driving force of the 'Emscher Park' – this work could not have been written. Consequently, the book is also a way of saying thank you to Karl Ganser.

Acknowledgements

I wish to thank my colleagues who helped me with the illustrations in this book.

International comparison of conurbations

The images of the area settlement are provided, with the kind consent of the publisher, by Klaus Humpert, Sibylle Becker and Klaus Brenner. *The Development of Metropolitan Agglomerations.*

In *Prozeß und Form 'natürlicher Konstruktion'* (Processes and Forms of 'Natural Construction'), edited by Klaus Teichmann and Joachim Wilke, Ernst und Sohn, Berlin, 1996, p. 182

The aerial photographs have kindly been provided by Prof. Eckard Ribbeck, Town Planning Institute of the University of Stuttgart and Prof. Kosta Mathey, Berlin.

Thirteen photos of Cologne

Photos and text on the 'Schäl Sick' of Cologne are by Boris Sieverts, born 1969, who, with interruptions, for ten years has been living on the right bank of the Rhine, the 'blind' Cologne Rhine bank. Boris Sieverts studied at the Academy of Art in Düsseldorf.

Gelsenkirchen Bismarck

The sequence of maps on the growth of the city quarter of Gelsenkirchen Bismarck has been compiled by the City of Gelsenkirchen, Town Planning Office, supervised by Michael von der Mühlen and Dr Heidemann.

The Rhine–Main Regional Park

The structural concept of the 'Rhine–Main Regional Park' was produced in 1994 at the request of the Umlandverband Frankfurt by Prof. Wolfgang Christ, Mediastadt, Darmstadt (www.mediastadt. com). The model project 'Rodau Regional Park' was produced to be implemented, based on the structural concept, by Barbara Boczek, of Topos, Darmstadt.

International Building Exhibition Emscher Park

The images of the projects of the International Building Exhibition Emscher Park have been put together by the Department of Publicity Relations, and I would like to thank in particular Mrs Sabine Radomski.

The city region of Stuttgart

The research study 'The City Region of Stuttgart' is compiled by Prof. Dr Roland Wick, Stuttgart/Darmstadt and is part of a joint lecture manuscript by Thomas Sieverts and Roland Wick.

Chapter 1

The living space of the majority of mankind

An anonymous space with no visual quality

Since the railway, car and electronics have exploded the spatial limits imposed by the muscular capabilities of human beings and animals, the city has been extending almost without restraint into the countryside. Its expansion and the degree of its dispersal follow the relevant traffic and communications technologies: the railway results in a star-shaped, linear expansion, the car fills in the surfaces and electronics leads to 'borderless' expansions. However, this development is based not only on technical inventions but also on far-reaching historical causes. The forces which produced the compact city and kept it together for 150 to 200 generations – by which I mean the priest-kings and religious associations, temples and churches, walls and markets, feudalism and the guilds – had definitively come to an end before these technical inventions.

It is possible that the compact city is itself only an interlude in the development of human civilisation. According to interpretations of the theory of evolution, human beings are primates, social animals living in loose groups who prefer life in the wide-open savannah and at the edge of light forests. The compact, walled city would therefore be an historically imposed form which would dissolve 'naturally' the moment the causal social forces are taken away.

Against this it might be argued from the perspective of cultural history that the cultural development of mankind in the past 5,000 years was inseparably connected with the development of the compact city. As result, it is part of the essence of human beings as cultural beings and with its dissolution the cultural development of humanity might also be jeopardised.

The dispute as to whether the disappearance of walls and moats around 1800 was a liberation or a loss of uniqueness and safety is as old as the event itself. Many citizens felt that through the opening up of the city to the open countryside they were being exposed to anxiety, whereas others greeted the liberation from narrowness and constraint. Goethe was one of those who welcomed the opening of the city:

> Even relatively large cities are now pulling down their walls, the moats even of princely castles are being filled in, cities are only large blotches, and if you see such a thing on your travels you think general peace is confirmed and the Golden Age is at the door. Nobody feels comfortable in a garden which does not look like open countryside; there should be no reminders of art or constraint, we want to be completely free to breathe the air without restriction.[2]

Whatever the reaction of citizens at the time may have been, it must be recorded that throughout the whole world the 'city' of the modern age extends into its environment and thus creates the peculiar forms of an urbanised landscape or a landscaped city.

Following a venerable tradition we still call distinct regions of settlement 'cities'. Or we describe them with such abstract concepts as 'city agglomerations', 'areas of concentration', 'urbanised landscapes', etc., because we note how inappropriate the concept of 'city' is when applied to these fields of settlement as they evoke completely different associations. For want of a better term, we shall call these structures which consist of 'fields' of various uses, construction forms and topographies *Zwischenstädte*. They take up large areas, and they have both urban and rural characteristics. The *Zwischenstadt* stands between the individual, special place as a geographical and historical event and ubiquitous developments of the global division of labour; between the space as an immediate living area and the abstract traversing of distance which is only measured in the consumption of time; between the mythical Old City which is still very effective, and the Old Cultural Landscape which remains anchored deep in our dreams.

The *Zwischenstadt* as an international phenomenon

This *Zwischenstadt*, which is neither city nor landscape, but which has characteristics of both, neither has a suitable name nor is it concrete. Despite the fact that it has no name, it can be found all over the world. Intermediate cities with 20–30 million inhabitants have emerged in Asia and South America. For all the massive differences, depending on the state of economic development, culture and topography, they have the shared feature that they have almost nothing to do with the relevant local pre-industrial urban traditions. Across all cultures of the entire world, they share specific common characteristics: a structure of completely different urban environments which at first sight is diffuse and disorganised with individual islands of geometrically structured patterns, a structure without a clear centre, but therefore with many more or less sharply functionally specialised areas, networks and nodes.

We find *Zwischenstädte* of this kind particularly conspicuous in areas in which cities grow beyond their own extensions into a city cluster, but most clearly where the historical, traditional city-composing forces never really took effect, such as in the Ruhr area, or also in the metropolitan areas of the Third World. In the *Zwischenstadt* the ratio of open landscape and built-up areas has frequently been reversed; the landscape has changed from being an all-inclusive 'background' to being a contained 'figure'. Conversely, the settlement surface has increased in size and openness and has acquired something of the character of a surrounding landscape. This *Zwischenstadt* is a field of living which, depending on one's interest and perspective, can be interpreted either as city or as country. Although the causes of this diffuse form may differ, they share the feature that the historical city-forming forces and the limits imposed by them had reached their end.

The Zwischenstadt *as a result of innumerable individual rational decisions*

As a whole, the diffuse city gives an 'unplanned' impression, but it has arisen out of innumerable individual, and – considered on their own – rational decisions. A typical example from an old industrial region might run as follows: a road exists, a factory is built, either because agricultural products are to be processed or because mineral resources are available, the processing of which might supply a growing market. The factory attracts worker settlements to it, and gardens are allocated to the workforce to enhance its self-sufficiency. The population next needs schools and shops. The growing employment and consumption market attracts further institutions and, as the social richness increases, a basis is formed for new specialisation and further division of labour. New traffic routes and public establishments become necessary, and in this way the evolution of the city continues on the principle of 'settlement creates settlement', without following any pattern planned in advance.

Another example, but coming from the Third World, may be that: an old city functions as a centre of attraction for city migrants who leave their villages for the widest possible range of reasons – usually there are several – ranging from overpopulation or lack of basic foodstuffs, caused by unemployment, to the promise of emancipation offered by migration to urban centres. Such migrants look for a place of settlement in which they have access to the blessings of the city but can still operate a modest semi-urban agricultural economy. The consequence of these decisions, each of which is logical in its own terms, is a less structured, more open settlement between city and country, which develops further with its own workplaces and facilities into a more or less independent *Zwischenstadt*.

Structurally comparable results are produced by the behaviour of house buyers in our cities. They are looking for properties which they can still afford, from which the core of the city can still easily be reached and at the same time access is open to the country. The consequence of such an accumulation of decisions, each cogent in itself, is the 'settled' landscape, which initially is almost exclusively residential and, after a period of intensification and consolidation, attracts workplaces and consumer provision. Only then does it develop into a *Zwischenstadt* which frees itself from its original dependency, supplies itself and enters into a relationship of mutual exchanges with the original city.

Statistical analysis in Germany shows that it is not so much the small towns, the central places prescribed for this purpose by town planning, which attract new inhabitants, but rural communities on the periphery of the 'central places'. From a forecast of the Federal Research Institute for Regional and National Development it is apparent that the borders of today's settlements, according to a conservative estimate, will expand by a further 10 per cent by 2010 (against a core growth of only about 2–4 per cent). 'It is becoming increasingly obvious that the residential environment is becoming more and more decisive for where we live and no longer, as in the past, the proximity of the workplace.'[3]

In the USA a similar development is taking place on a much larger scale; the triggers in many cases are motorway exits, major shopping centres and, for several years now, major office complexes on motorway intersections. These are at the same time the consequences and causes of settlement activity. Also these very widespread *Zwischenstädte* have long since separated themselves from the original city, but here the dependency relationship has often been reversed – the impoverished core city now looks for its work places in the surrounding *Zwischenstadt*.[4]

Even in cases in which the planning of major interconnected urban expansions offer possibilities for strong concentration, these newly planned urban configurations are rather uniform, only marginally centralised and differentiated, because the configurations of day-to-day living are relatively diffuse and changing.[5]

In the sequence of the development of the *Zwischenstadt*, internationally comparable stages are apparent.

> After a phase of rapid urbanisation, accelerated by migration between country and city, there is usually a slower phase, in which the surplus birth rate is normally the main cause of growth. In still later phases, as is apparent in Western Europe, the annual growth of the city falls to below 1 per cent, and the rate of immigration increases again. This also conceals the consequences of excess ageing in the cities and the emigration of families with small children and the prosperous to the attractive surrounding small towns and villages.'[6]

Over time, the original freedom of the choice of location becomes increasingly restricted. The area fills up, new developments have to respond to a context which is becoming more and more built-up and constricted. At some stage, the available land is fully developed, the *Zwischenstadt* has 'grown-up', and further development can and may only be implemented through intensification, reutilisation and the regeneration of disused sites. Old urban fabric and uses become superfluous, they are converted, reused, rebuilt and finally removed. All this taken together produces a carpet of settlement which appears to be without any plan but has the nature of a palimpsest in which old, superfluous and deleted text and images glimmer through the new text.

The unique character of the Zwischenstadt

Urban development in different parts of the world is subjected to very different forces. Whereas urban expansion in the Ruhr, Wallonia and the English Midlands is directed by heavy industry, in countries such as India, Africa and South America it is subject to the pressures of overpopulated rural areas. In the USA and Western Europe trends follow the investment of wealth in private residential areas or the compulsion towards affordable housing on inexpensive land. Despite the massive differences in the forces behind urban development, the result in each case is the diffuse form of the *Zwischenstadt*, which separates itself from the core city – if one still exists – and achieves a unique form of independence.

These characteristics link the area of Greater Tokyo with the Ruhr area, São Paulo with Boswash – the area between Boston and Washington in the USA which has merged into an integrated city environment – and Mexico City with Bombay. Even the area of Greater Stuttgart or the Rhine–Main area could be characterised in this way. Major differences are based on the varying densities of residential and car use. The *Zwischenstädte* in the Third World are on the whole still denser and more compact than the more dispersed forms in the industrialised world. When compared with the giant *Zwischenstädte* in Asia and South America, comprising more than 20 million people, perhaps we should regard the increase in areas of concentration in European Countries as one single *Zwischenstadt*.[7]

What Karl Ganser says about the Emscher region applies to all cities across the whole world as soon as they have grown beyond the size of small major cities or, indeed, have formed in a period in which historical city-forming forces were no longer effective.

As, for example, in the Ruhr area:

This 800 sq. km large settlement area . . . is essentially fully developed. It is a *Zwischenstadt*, which does not correspond to our ordinary image of the city and our yearning for an intact landscape. With the weak growth potential of the time ahead of us, this settlement structure can no longer be reconfigured. We must assume that it is a given and develop its hidden qualities.'[8]

In all intermediate cities, characteristic patterns of interpenetration of open spaces and built form have become apparent. A generally common characteristic of the *Zwischenstadt* is the continued search for the implementation of the 'Tucholsky principle', the simultaneous yearning for both the urban and rural ideal which he describes in one of his famous poems entitled 'The Ideal'. The Tucholsky principle is the search for reconciliation between the contrasts of participation in human society, the life of the city, and participation in nature. In other words, it is the yearning for a combination of pastoral romanticism and the comforts of the city.[9] This search for a resolution to the underlying paradox of a combination between urban centrality and contact with the countryside was also shared by the early socialists Owen and Fourier, by the reformers Cerdá and Howard and by the visionary architects Frank Lloyd Wright, Le Corbusier and Hilberseimer.[10] It is also still being pursued by innumerable home and land owners in day-to-day practice and is leading to a maximisation of the interface between built-up area and the countryside. These boundaries are of particular ecological interest and fit in well with the 'primate nature' of man. In the last few years they have excited the interest of 'fractal researchers' who have attempted to represent these growth processes in mathematical terms, with extremely interesting results.[11] They show how, at the macro level of the city region, growth processes and the distribution of the different sizes of settlements occur quite similarly in major agglomerations throughout the world and how similar the developments appear at different levels of scale. These patterns form virtually independent of the political, cultural and socio-economic backgrounds.

In Germany, these settlement patterns have been characterised by the particular form of local authority self-administration – with heavy competition between communes.

The developments have been driven by immigration and segregation against which town planning is powerless. At the same time, these are the problem areas which result from the decisions of the inhabitants which affect them most directly. This means that definitions of the problems of urban development would more sensibly be concentrated on not denying these trends but rather by accepting them as critical conditions for the development of the problem.

In addition, the developments are based on the fact that the local authorities each have to pursue their own interests. Their competition forms the basis for the tendency to exploit the advantages of the peripheral location against the settlement centres and to plan for residential and commercial areas which only drive forward the process of settlement expansion with all its consequences. Against this, city development planning is powerless – at least as long as it conceives itself as 'local authority development planning'. It will not be able do anything else until such time as the local authorities in the agglomeration areas merge into political units (and not only sectoral specialist associations). For this purpose, however, they must largely give up or restrict their political existence; but this cannot be expected from them.'[12]

However, planning across local authority boundaries is restricted due to sovereignty and public expenditure limits. Simultaneously, with the restriction of public funds for publicly subsidised housing, infrastructure and public facilities, urban and regional planning is losing one of its last instruments for an effective, active influence on the evolution of urban areas.

Zwischenstadt *and landscape*

Whereas obvious, though sometimes politically and culturally modified international comparisons can be observed at the macro level of the *Zwischenstadt*, there are clear differences at the micro level of the three-dimensional urban structure caused by cultural and socio-economic factors. These can be classified among the theoretical models for the 1920s and 1930s as being between the *Ville Radieuse* of Le Corbusier (or the 'Big City Architecture' of the early Hilberseimer) on the one hand, and Wright's Broadacre

City (or Hilberseimer's later diagrams for US cities) on the other. The grain and density of development of the individual urban areas and the degree of penetration with open spaces and landscapes determine the specific character of each *Zwischenstadt*. Thus, whereas large Asian cities are tending more and more strongly towards Hilberseimer's type of 'Big City Architecture' and the US major cities are polarising between 'Big City Architecture' and Broadacre City, Europe's main cities mostly constitute mixed forms in the manner of the *Ville Radieuse* and Broadacre City. The *Zwischenstadt* can develop any diversity of settlement and built form, so long as, as a whole, they are intelligible in their settlement network and, above all, remain embedded as an 'archipelago' in the 'sea' of an interconnected landscape. In this way the landscape becomes the glue of the *Zwischenstadt*. In assessing and evaluating the character of this sort of landscape, perspectives on the *Zwischenstadt* differ: if we take the large 'consumption of landscape' or 'transformation of landscape' as an argument against the *Zwischenstadt*, one must bear in mind the fact that not only in the Garden City, but particularly in the compact city, the open space is always regarded as an indispensable complementary component, even in cases in which its character has changed from being the necessary source of food into an area for ecological balance or a place for recreation.

Even cities with a large number of inhabitants, such as Shanghai or Calcutta have, until recently – thanks to very high residential and occupation densities – remained so restricted in their extent that every day they could be supplied from the country with handcarts and wagons laden with fresh goods. The city area of Mexico City (approximately 20 million inhabitants) is the same as that of Berlin (3.5 million inhabitants).[13] In almost all parts of the Berlin of the nineteenth century, landscape was present in the form of small allotments only a walking or cycling distance from the densely inhabited residential areas. Once we take these into consideration, the densities of different cities and neighbourhoods which, at first glance, seemed so exceptionally different, become relative. Even the 'Märkische Viertel' in Berlin, by our standards a very dense, high-rise peripheral estate of the 1960s, has a rather moderate overall density if we allow for the recreational areas and open spaces which are intrinsically associated with it.

In-built redundancy versus capacity to adjust and the conservation of resources?

Special conditions of our mature industrial societies apply to the *Zwischenstadt*, on the one hand, low densities of activity and, on the other, freedom in the location of functions. The density of occupation is low and the building mass is comparatively large. Viewed in rational economic terms, we already have too much built fabric, which is used only for relatively short periods of the day and of the year. The question therefore arises whether, in the long-term, we will be able to meet the running costs, the costs of energy consumption, ongoing maintenance, repairs and renovation or whether we will have to find more economic forms of the *Zwischenstadt* because of this excess load on the economy. With the demise of location-dependent heavy industry and the increase of services, dependence on specific locations has relaxed significantly, thanks above all to the availability of good roads and communication networks. Therefore the location pattern of building fabric, of functions and of open space can, in principle, be selected freely. Thus, functions and structures can develop in response to the different natural and cultural characteristics of the region and in response to different socio-economic conditions (prices and charges) and socio-cultural challenges (lifestyle, purchasing power). The latter are changing profoundly.

Reduced working times, blocks of several days of free time during the working week, abbreviated working lifetimes in the form of 'early retirement' or 'training years' and working from home, are affecting the patterns of travel times between living 'in the country' and 'working in the city'. This will promote a further spatial separation of work and living places rather than a mixture of uses, except for specific services in the medium-sized economy.

These developments are causing a further expansion of, and the segregation of land uses in, the *Zwischenstadt*. This could have the effect that the resulting urban structures due to their major transport costs, consumption of resources and mono-functional, unilaterally determined land uses – can no longer adapt to a profound structural change caused by an ecological crisis.

Increased freedom for the location of functions in the city would, with the support of microelectronics, permit mixed and intensified urban structures in which the use of all the possibilities of telecommunications would reduce the transport volume and engender a more settled way of life. The *Zwischenstadt* would indeed make it possible to develop such urban structures, but this would presuppose a different lifestyle. The question remains open as to whether and how we would be able to prepare our cities for such a structural change and the drastically reduced consumption of resources which would result.

For whatever reasons, in the future about half of the population of the world will live in *Zwischenstädten*. These structures are often so large, in some cases with 10 to 30 million people, that their inhabitants have no opportunity whatever to escape them in their day-to-day living. As a result, all the living requirements, including the production of food in an urban farming economy, must exist within these *Zwischenstädten*. The urban areas in the *Zwischenstadt* must also meet all the requirements of an ecological balance, since there will be no other areas to offset any imbalance.

The fate of the *Zwischenstadt* is shared by all humanity, and in this regard no country has an 'inborn' advantage. Every culture can learn from the others. The distinctions into the First, Second and Third World become increasingly harmful, and it is we Europeans who must give up the arrogant role of the teacher and enter into a dialogue in which we are prepared to learn from other cultures.[14] This applies in particular to those economic and ecological conditions of scarcity to which Europe will have to adjust either voluntarily or amid catastrophes brought on by the necessity of adjusting to the rightful amount of global resources it is entitled to. The globalisation of the economy is changing the world into a system of communicating tubes. Exporting jobs and capital is inevitably connected with the importation of poverty, which will force us to alter our lifestyle drastically. In the foreseeable future, the borders between poor and rich will no longer be between north and south, but across all the cities of the world, and Europe will not be exempt.

Despite the worldwide distribution of the *Zwischenstadt*, when confronted with it as a political and design-task, all cultures find it a problem which so far appears to be insoluble and lack any strategy. There are several reasons for this:

- The *Zwischenstadt* does not have an independent identity either in the imagination of its occupants or as a subject for politics.

- The shaping of the *Zwischenstadt* can no longer be achieved by the traditional resources of town planning, urban design and architecture. New ways must be explored, which are as yet unclear.
- Last but not least, the fascination of the myth of the Old City clouds our view of the reality of the periphery.

The obstruction of our view by the myth of the Old City

In view of the massive and constantly accelerating expansion of the cities' built-up areas, there is a massive campaign in support of the traditional densely packed European city. This city, with its mixture of uses, its plot structure and its public spaces delineated by the walls of buildings is propagated as the immediately available and exclusive model for current urban design and development.[15]

There are good reasons supporting this view. In energy terms, the densely packed city is very favourable because of its relatively small surface area given its large construction volume. It optimises the utilisation of the built-up area, particularly so when uses with different daylight needs and different sensitivities can be mixed vertically on a single plot of land. Density and mixture also contribute to short travel distances. This mixture plus density leads in turn to an animation of the public space and to a richness of experience, especially for children. Last but not least, this diversity leads to an unambiguous, contrast-rich delineation between city and country.

Despite all these plausible advantages, today we can only reproduce this type of city or district in exceptional circumstances, so profoundly have the social, commercial, cultural and political parameters changed.

All attempts to translate the image and structural type of the historical European city more or less directly into a general model for the future are, in my opinion, destined to fail. Indeed, I will go further still. The task is not only to acknowledge this fact but with an appropriate element of regret, to bid farewell to this well-loved image, despite its inexhaustible cultural diversity and the resurgence in city tourism. However, we should be aware of the fact that the love of the Old City is a relatively new phenomenon which dates back only one generation.

The patterns of area settlement of conurbations

International comparison of conurbations exhibits characteristic differences as well as commonalities. Conurbations in the First World and in the Third World have extreme differences of density, numbers of inhabitants and are very different in extent. The Asiatic conurbations are the most compact, whereas the North American ones are the loosest. Despite these differences, all conurbations show a tendency to fray, to merge with the landscape.

Izmir, Turkey

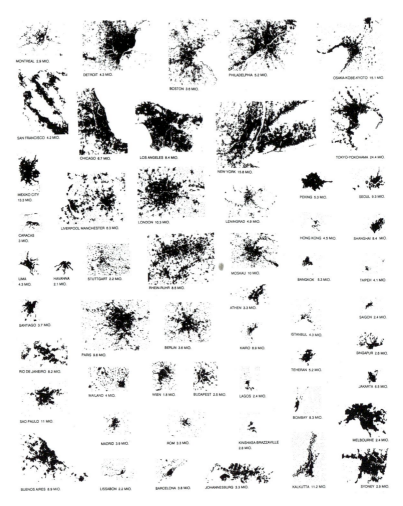

The area settlement patterns of 55 conurbations

Settlement sprawl, Mexico City

Settlement sprawl, Mexico City

Bidding farewell to the Old City, mourning it and consigning it to history also means committing ourselves to retain and protect these historic and irreparable characteristics of the city. Wherever possible we should at least do everything we can to maintain the existing Old City structure and endeavour to ensure that it is not eaten away internally, or emptied, by uses which will destroy its fabric, as is happening almost everywhere at present.

I can remember my astonishment and alarm when, in a planning study for a medieval city centre, we found that the proprietors of businesses in small Old City houses had removed the stairs on the ground floor in order to gain 3 square metres more retail area and 1.5 metres more shop window. The upper floors, now only reachable by rungs fixed to the external wall from the backyard, were standing empty, decorated with curtains and light in shifting patterns in order to imitate 'life'. Their utilisation was no longer profitable.[16] In a similar vein, a few years ago the retailers of the *Zeil* in the City of Frankfurt, the street in the Federal Republic with the highest volume of sales, offered to take over responsibility for the design and safety of the street, including relieving the police of the duty of surveillance.[17] Such trends towards a desertification of the inner cities must be fought.

In places where the particular cultural, social and economic conditions make it possible, we should promote new reforms of the densely mixed city, such as in the re-establishment of the Lower New City of Kassel.[18] But here we are dealing with the delayed reconstruction of an inner-city expansion on the basis of the historic city plan, a special case which can only be of general use if specific characteristics of our society, such as private and personal mobility, the distribution of employment and specialisation, the desire for proximity to nature and a large amount of private space, were to be reversed fundamentally across a broad spectrum of the population.

In practice, these approaches are useful only in exceptional cases; in the planning context of the *Zwischenstadt* they fail. Indeed, the one-sided love for the historical city is the main reason for our repression of the challenge presented by unloved suburbia.

The overpowering image of the Old City clouds our view of the reality of our modern cities, among which the historically formed city core only constitutes a small fraction. The power of the old image of the city is made strikingly clear by a mental experiment:

we cannot imagine a city which we know, indeed not even our own city, without its historical centre, although the inhabited area outside the historical centre may be at least ten times as large.

This inner fixation with the Old City promotes prejudices in the consideration and assessment of the suburbs and the periphery. Here we use, without careful observation, derogatory terms such as 'suburban sprawl', 'cancerous growth', 'over-development', 'consumption of landscape' and 'desert'.

This welter of prejudice clouds our view not only of the area of the suburban space of the *Zwischenstadt* but also of the present reality of the historical city centres themselves. If our gaze is fixed not only on the shell of the old historical façades but, as the example of the removed staircases shows, looks inside rather more closely, we find that the Old City becomes more and more like the shopping centres of the periphery. The competition with 'green field' shopping centres and high rents have the effect that essentially only branch stores, chain stores and high profit services can afford to locate in city cores. This means that the Old City, by selling bourgeois culture, has been more and more deprived of day-to-day features of living, handicrafts and trade as well as the special, the striking and the one-off character which it once had. With the assistance of city managers, the historical city changes into a quite ordinary shopping centre. The burden of the Old City as the identity bearer for the entire city region, increases to the same extent as the balance between core and city region shifts more and more in the direction of the city region. The identity structure of the Old City is overloaded and collapsing.[19]

For this reason, we should not love our Old City centres to death while we top them up with pseudo-historical buildings and overload them with supposedly urban functions, such as the promotion of retailing. This leads to their destruction. On the contrary, if we want to protect the Old City, residential use should be strengthened by all our resources. Furthermore, new urban places with 'city centre' functions should be created at other places in the city region in order to reduce the pressure on the historical core. These places represent an opportunity for the *Zwischenstadt* to develop its independence from the centre of the Old City.

If we are prepared to acknowledge and accept the city as the whole that it really is, and that is indeed the minimum requirement towards caring for it, we nostalgic Europeans must work our way through a set of concepts which are loaded with beautiful old images and test them for their present validity. We must throw away a whole raft of rhetorical debris in order to recreate access to the reality of the city. However, this involves simple things and actions, which we usually forget or suppress.

A review of the concepts

The following five concepts will be examined for their reliability as tools for understanding and intervening in the city. They all play an important role in the present discussion in planning theory and planning policy: urban-ness, centrality, density, mixed use and ecology. In a specific sense they sum up the 'good city'. All these concepts have a long history in the inventory of ideas. However, we will only make cursory reference to them here; what we are interested in is their current use.

These five key concepts are related to each other and, in the context of the discussion, cross-refer to each other, but it makes sense to look at them separately, because they each accentuate specific aspects of the discussion.

Urban-ness

The key concept of the discussion is urban-ness. The concept of urban-ness was developed in particular by Edgar Salin as a particular quality of the enlightened, bourgeois city and was coined to indicate a cultural and social form of living and not the quality of a specific form of urban design and spatial structure. By urban-ness he meant a tolerant, outward-looking attitude of its inhabitants, to each other and to outsiders.[20] Today, this concept is often narrowed to the image of the dense city of the nineteenth century; consequently a general loss of urban-ness is deplored and accordingly there is the demand for town planning and urban design to have more concern for urban-ness. However, even in this general discussion, there is also a rather flatter and vaguer, nonetheless suggestive, concept of social urban-ness in play. Urban-ness in this case acts as a kind of counter-concept to provincialness by evoking an atmosphere of cosmopolitanism, openness to the world and tolerance, intellectual agility and curiosity. However, this social concept is connected in the imagination too closely with the image of commercial bustle on the streets, squares and markets, with coffee houses flowing with stimulating discussions, with the attractive and diverse range of multifarious goods and services. It is not closely enough associated with a specific cosmopolitan way of life. The deficit is perceived in the *image* of the city. As a result the lack of a dense and bustling street life or 'lived' urban-ness, is often confused with the 'constructed' urban-ness of streets with continuous façades, squares and avenues.

This type of urban-ness is predominantly historically defined. It is based not so much on social and political qualities as on an idealised image of the bourgeois European city of the late eighteeth and nineteenth centuries, recorded in travelogues and novels. The early social science studies of Simmel and others, however, took a thoroughly critical view of this type of urban-ness.[21] We might deplore the concept of urban-ness becoming a shallow image, but this still has a powerful influence. Nowadays, this ideal image is purified of beggars and thieves, of stocks and gallows, which contributed at least as much to the jolly bustle in markets and squares. It is the image of a chemically purified urban-ness.

The street scenes recorded in the travel descriptions of the eighteenth and nineteenth centuries present us with a density of street life which today is almost unimaginable and which, in Central Europe, we only experience at the major popular festivals, such as the Edinburgh Festival or the Oktoberfest in Munich. We can also experience urban-ness in the form of dense streets and street life in developing countries, where it is still in its pre-industrial character. This type of urban-ness is a core component of the booming city tourism and it is here that it becomes strikingly clear that the pre-industrial form of urban-ness can be read as the expression of a specific historical socio-economic condition or retrospection. No Central European would like to spend long following such a lifestyle.

An entertaining impression of the severity of life, urban density and mixture of use in my home city of Hamburg in the seventeenth century is given by a description in the 'Elbschwanenbüchlein' (The Booklet of Swans on the Elbe) by the local Baroque poet and 'Imperial Count Palatine' of Wedel, Johann Rist (1606–1667):

When during this last war I had to spend some time in the world-famous city of Hamburg, I experienced the great difference between living in the city and in the country. I lived in one of the most distinguished streets, in the entire city. In this street, there was a constant toing and froing of horses, carts and wagons, early and late. They often met head on and, because of the narrowness of the street, could not get past each other, so that the drivers swore appallingly. So much so that I, who was living right next to the street, often thought that the roofs of the houses would collapse and strike down and crush such blasphemers. In the large and spacious house in which I was living, sugar was boiled, which created a lot of activity, particularly since the servants, both night and day, constantly made an incessant hubbub taking the sugar up and down the stairs. My next-door neighbour to the right was a goldsmith and, to the left, lived a coppersmith. The latter was having some building work done in his home. It is easy to imagine the frantic activities of the carpenters all day long, but the hammering and tapping of the goldsmith and coppersmith from early morning to late in the evening could easily have driven you quite mad. Right opposite me lived a spur maker, whose filing and scrubbing made my head sometimes so sore that I often wished that he and all his rasps were sitting in the market place of Augsburg. Worst of all for me, due to a serious thigh injury which I received in an unexpected accident, I had to stay in bed most of the time with an unbelievable pain, so that for many weeks I was not able to get out of the house at all. Consequently, when I finally got out of the city and back to my own patch, although I found the place devastated, sacked and plundered, I thought that I come from hell to heaven so oppressive had I found the bustle of the city.'[22]

Cramped residential and working conditions and their consequences illustrate the other side of the coin. This is how life in the beautiful, romantic destinations of city tourism in the Third World today, and even the lively street and bar life in the European cities of the nineteenth century, can be seen. Who among us would be happy to have to emerge from a cramped and overcrowded home onto the street as our only open space and have to take refuge in a bar as an extended drawing-room? To put it another way, the loss of urban-ness of the type taking place in our Central European cities is a direct consequence of vastly improved residential and employment conditions which enable us to carry out in our homes, offices and workshops, many activities previously allocated to the public or semi-public realm. The loss of urban-ness for us goes hand-in-hand with the liberalisation of narrow, constricting social control and with the gaining of greater individual areas of freedom and development. The loss is therefore part of our emancipation from commercial, social and natural constraints. This emancipation has its ecological and its social price, and we cannot know precisely how long we will have to go on paying it. The liberation from the old historical constraints has so far led to a continuing spatial dilution of social activity. In the course of one generation the amount of area per urban resident and employee has at least doubled, alone the residential area per person has been increasing in the last few decades by at least half a square metre per year per person. Increasing wealth will be invested to a large extent in privately owned space. If, however, we wish to compare the present residential and employment density with conditions in the nineteenth century, at that time it was up to four or five times higher, bringing it close to the present densities of cities in the Third World. This dilution of spontaneous social contact is also made strikingly clear by the observation that the probability of children today randomly chancing upon others of the same age for games on the street is usually so low that they have to find other forms of meeting and playing together. They make their arrangements on the telephone.

This is also why the social significance of public space as a meeting space for people has declined so much in our time. Public space is hardly needed any longer for our existence. It is now only occasionally needed for the odd demonstration and although for these purposes it is irreplaceable, it sometimes functions as a political meeting place or a place for expressing solidarity. But all other activities which were earlier located in the public space have emigrated to large and comfortable residences and workplaces; to social institutions; to specialised institutions such as clubs and leisure facilities and to shops and department stores. The mutual neighbourly assistance, which was necessary for survival, has been replaced by insurance policies against fire, illness and emergency which operate across society. Irrespective of the density, today's city residents choose their social contacts less on the basis of proximity and neighbourhood than on interests and inclinations which are not governed by space.

The development towards trans-local orientation could be somewhat slowed down by a slowing down of the expansion of the road network and through a sharp increase in the cost of car travel, thereby giving spatial proximity a greater value. But this overall trend cannot be reversed. Much would already have been achieved if floor areas of buildings were used to capacity through a timing of different activities. By this means alone density of utilisation and the potential for encounter would be increased. However, despite the loss of immediate social significance, despite the dilution of uses and trans-local orientation, public space remains the basic structural framework of the *Zwischenstadt*. Only through public space can it be perceived and understood and, as a tool of experience and sign of identity, public space is more important than ever for the intelligibility and legibility of the *Zwischenstadt*.

The image of old urban-ness and its public space is still so attractive that for several decades it has been artificially instigated, for example, to create a propensity for shopping in the pedestrian zones of inner-city and peripheral shopping centres. The everyday world is put on the stage![23]

If the unbroken power of attraction of shopping centres seems to reveal a hunger for urban-ness, and if we do not feel satisfied with this retailer-instigated urban-ness, what practical meaning can this concept still have today? What aspects of its wide-ranging meaning are still relevant for the city of today and tomorrow? For it seems that we do not want to give up the concept of urban-ness even in a purified form, because if that were to happen, a major and essential characteristic of the European city would be given up completely. Consequently, we must seek new forms and spaces for urban-ness.

Here it is necessary to point out that such qualities as cosmopolitanism and an openness to the world, intellectual volatility, tolerance and curiosity are not tied to specific historically structured forms of space but can arise in other spatial contexts, which are openly accessible and possess room and atmosphere for encounters. These are the spaces which the US social philosopher Michael Walzer wants to call *open-minded spaces* (as opposed to *single-minded spaces*). In this sense, many American university campuses exceed our inner cities in urban-ness! On the other hand, when you look more closely at markets and squares, there are forms of interaction in the public space, in street cafés and in popular festivals which can be attributed urban qualities, if we do not set the cultural benchmarks too high. It is necessary for suitable spatial and functional arrangements to promote and support, if not to produce, these forms of interaction.

Perhaps, it must be accepted as inevitable, but also as an opportunity for urban cultural policy, that urban-ness must be staged, i.e. that urban-ness today requires special occasions to be able to make itself manifest. However, this task should not be entrusted to retailers, but should be taken seriously as an indispensable part of cultural and sports policy, to involve people who would not normally be reached. In Central Europe, urban-ness has developed from being an existential factor of life into being an objective to be shaped by cultural means. Perhaps, in addition to theatre producers there must also be city producers who stage events in the public spaces of the city.[24] We do not want to end up with a complete 'festivalisation' of politics in which those policy areas that cannot be staged effectively, are neglected. 'The city as a stage' should not overshadow the two other concepts of 'the city as a workshop' and 'the city as a home'.[25]

There is, of course, another well-developed and industrially structured culture with a high standard of living in which – admittedly in a quite different form – we can still find forms of old urban-ness: in the Japanese major city. There, in one of the richest industrial nations in the world, the residential and employment conditions, due to extremely high land prices, remain so constrained that many of the activities that for us are typically domestic, albeit declining, still take place in the public space or in semi-public institutions.[26] For example, bathing, eating, receiving friends, entertainment, even making love can now all take place in dedicated semi-public areas in a form that is in some cases thoroughly luxurious. Could this formulation of urban-ness be a model for us? I am rather sceptical about that because, even in Japan with its rising standard of living, these uses of space are on the wane. The principle of the shifting of specific functions from the home to the public space will be investigated in connection with the concept of mixed use.

Centrality

Closely connected with the concept of urban-ness is the concept of centrality. The term 'central' extends beyond a merely geometrical meaning, to function as an alternative expression for significant, important, powerful. The idea of a centre is intended to designate a place in which everything important can be found and from which all major developments start.

It is possible that in a metaphorical sense our inner orientation functions also in the form of 'central places', where we store our knowledge in order to find it again. Almost every form of traditional order works with classified, hierarchical levels. The official planning system in Germany, for example, is based on a coordinated pyramid-shaped system of central places. The system of the cities and the centres in the cities is interpreted, and normatively planned, as a classical hierarchical tree structure. This also complies with the image of an ordered, well-structured society, fitting in with the equally hierarchically arranged administrative structures.

The classification of cities in accordance with a hierarchically developed principle of central places of differing ranks means their subjugation under an idealised principle of order. In the pre-industrial period – and indeed until far into the industrial period – it made many things simpler and was a rational instrument for national planning. Today, however, it is outmoded for the reality behind the concept of the centre and of centrality has already largely disappeared and been attributed to other structures. For a long time cities have not been organised in an hierarchical 'tree structure', instead the system should be interpreted as a network with nodes.[27]

In such a network, all elements can ideally be co-equal, and there is no prioritising hierarchy. Each part of the city can take on specific central tasks, i.e. tasks occurring only uniquely or at least not ubiquitously, and in another respects it can retain thoroughly ubiquitous characteristics. However, this typologically ideal constellation applies to our cities only on an exceptional basis; usually, we still have to deal with pronounced central formations of different types, and that is a good thing.

However, for several reasons and for a considerable time the trend in the evolution of our cities has been towards the dismantling of spatially centralised hierarchies in favour of more evenly distributed specialisation in terms of the division of labour and the function of space.

The city structure is changing quietly and surreptitiously and extending into the surrounding countryside. Inevitably it loses its familiar historical character and its reassuring legibility between the poles of 'centre' and 'periphery'. With the dissolution of the concept of the 'centre', that of the 'periphery' also loses its conceptual content, in particular because the periphery is enriching itself with a wide range of different kinds of centres.

This development is sometimes subjected to severe criticism as it allegedly leads to the undermining of the centre, intensifies the growth of settlements into the countryside and blurs the demarcation.[28] For this reason, politicians and administrators seek to offset this change, without being able to halt this excessively powerful trend driven by the competition between the cities for more than a temporary period.

A *Zwischenstadt* of a more network-like structure will no longer have one large functional centre, but numerous functionally and symbolically diversified centres which will mutually supplement each other and, when taken together, make up the essence of the city. However, this also conceals the danger of mistakes and inappropriate developments. At present, the trend is towards ever larger, mono-functional and specialised shopping and leisure centres with insulated internal worlds located within a huge separating desert of car parks.[29] Without the integration of day-to-day functions in the centres, and without access by means other than the car, the city will become almost uninhabitable for many women, for children, for teenagers and for the old and the handicapped, because the majority of the population has – even if this is again and again expressed – no car available. Therefore politics must seek to minimise use of the car.

Today the question about the essence of an appropriate centrality and centre requires a new answer. The single centre, in which all the major institutions of the city as a whole are combined, will no longer exist. Nevertheless each city requires a centre that represents the essence of the city. Paradoxically such a centre will, in a time of functional change, become more stable and significant the less it is connected functionally and the more powerfully it is symbolically charged with a wider range of meanings and an open capacity for various interpretations. A good example of this,

although not from the *Zwischenstadt*, is the ruin of the Kaiser
Wilhelm Memorial Church in Berlin, which – although of minor
architectural value and without any real function – is the undisputed centre of the western part of the city, precisely because it is
effectively functionless and for that reason can convey a broad
spectrum of meaning. This became particularly apparent when the
architect Egon Eiermann produced his modern church with its
modern tower next to it and obviously wanted to tear down the
old, useless and ugly ruin. There was widespread protest through
all sections of the population, although only the very old could
associate the name of the church with the Imperial Era. For the
generations of those today over 60 years of age, it was and still is
the last memorial of the war and the nights of bombing. For those
who are now in their forties and fifties it is a sign of the period of
post-war reconstruction and for those still younger it signifies the
last non-commercialised 'place of freedom' in the middle of a business area. Consequently, in the 1960s, it was occupied by hippies
and flower people and it is still a favourite meeting place for the
young and the dispossessed.

Density

The third most important concept in connection with urban-ness
and centrality and only detachable from them for analytical purposes is density. A condensed urban form is again in demand especially in the last few years. The argument of the majority of
planners is that only with compact development can urbanity be
combined with limited settlement expansion for the protection of
the countryside.[30]

  This demand, although at first sight so attractive, must be met
with scepticism, because it is based on a whole series of untested
assumptions. In town planning discussions, the concept of density
is frequently employed but remains rather undifferentiated. In this
discussion we have to draw a clear distinction between material
density (the mass of building volume and floor space per built-up
area), visual-spatial density (the degree of the discernible spatial
enclosure) and the social density (the quantity and quality of possible social contacts per unit of settlement). These three dimensions of density only correlate with one another under certain
conditions; the discrepancy between spatial and social density has

already been referred to in the discussion of urban-ness. Specific forms of high material density tend to diminish the frequency and quality of social contacts as in, for example, the concentration of many flats around the core of vertical circulation in a high-rise building.

There is even little evidence for a direct relationship between material and perceived visual-spatial density. Lower buildings permit shorter distances between building frontages and therefore more intimate spatial structures. The secret in spatial and design terms of the much loved medieval city resides in the fact that the enclosed space of the narrow and treeless streets was complemented by broad, inner areas used as parks or for gardening, which were only later filled up. The original density of the medieval city was actually quite moderate. In specific cases a direct relationship can be applied between perceived visual-spatial and social density, if the houses are orientated towards the shared social space, the street. The social quality is thus less closely connected with the absolute density than with the spatial organisation.[31]

In yet another major context, the ecologically sensitive integration of the city into the countryside, the majority of planners demand high-density development because it is only with high density, so they argue, that the consumption of the countryside can be restricted. This is a widely held argument which nevertheless is only true to a limited extent. Indeed, it has been known since the 1920s that the intensification of urban development only makes sense up to a certain moderate limit above which it hardly contributes to the saving of areas and causes instead a deterioration of the quality of the residential environment.

The reasons for this are very simple. The living area occupied by each inhabitant consists on average of about 40–50 per cent of a settlement's overall area. The rest is used for employment, traffic, services and facilities. If, with such a pattern of land use, the average density of residential occupation was to be increased by half, only about 10–12 per cent of the overall settlement area would be saved and this would be at the price of the most humanly sensitive areas of the city, the residential. With increasing development density, the amount saved decreases and is more and more open to question. This is not, however, a plea for free-standing detached houses, but for a thoroughly moderate intensification, as we see for example in the density achieved through low-rise terraced houses with small plots of land or blocks of flats of three or four storeys.

A moderate increase in the density of development, specifically in the *Zwischenstadt*, from a current average plot ratio (gross floor area to plot size) of 0.2–0.3 for detached family houses to 0.4–0.6 for terraced and semi-detached houses would lead to an effective halving of the required building land without compromising expectations of quality.[32]

Most planners believe that increasing the density of urban development is necessary for the preservation of land. This is, however, a problematic argument, because it immediately involves several conflicts. Ecological balance on the development site itself can only be achieved with a plot ratio of up to 0.8 maximum. If the density grows beyond this, the ground has to be completely built over because of parking space needed. However, due to a growing shortage of development sites and escalating land prices, the principle of keeping a moderate density that makes it possible to reduce interference with the natural habitat on the site finds itself more and more in conflict with the requirement for much higher development densities in order to use sites sparingly and economically.

In Germany the conflict is well illustrated in the National Planning Code of 1st July 1987. In the first paragraph of section 5, under 9, the target is set out that there should be an economical and considerate use of land, an objective with which everyone would agree. However, on closer inspection, as soon as the two expressions are taken literally, difficulties appear. How, for example, is the requirement of the code to be viewed if, through high development density, the amount of land needed for development is minimised but, as a result of this high density, the site is completely built over and no natural ground remains? Are we then not dealing with the conflicting notions of 'saving sites that might be built on' but 'destroying the ground on which we build'? Conversely, employing a moderate development density could have a light footprint but would not save 'potential development land'. In this case, the conflicting notions of 'preserving the ground on a site' but 'wasting development land' would apply.

This concept from the German National Planning Code is obviously at odds with itself. The reason for this is that, despite their shared ecological objectives, the concepts have different origins. The promotion of a form of development which saves land is older. It goes back to the discussions on urban sprawl, the large-scale consumption of land and to the old debate on the optimal utilisation of the infrastructure. It is also a consequence of rising land prices. In this context 'sites' and 'land' should be seen rather in the macro-dimension of 'development areas' and the 'country-side'. However, the promotion of development that saves land has not only ecological but also rural–aesthetic dimensions and economic undertones. The call for a mode of development which has a light footprint is more recent. It goes back to the discussion which focuses on the notion of 'ground' and 'soil'. In the public discussion, both concepts are based on the now popular but negative slogan of the 'consumption of the countryside'. This idea seems to be attractive and readily combines with the equally popular slogans of 'development as environmental destruction', the 'suburban deserts' and the 'concrete jungle'.

The concepts of 'light footprint' and 'development which saves land' are in themselves not very helpful, unless they are further qualified. Both, redefined respectively as the economical use of land and the considerate use of the site, derive quite clearly from the wider field of the ecological debate, but their obvious incompatibility points to the fundamentally unresolved conflict within the ecology movement itself.[33] The Swiss deal with the tension between the two concepts with the beautiful notion of 'good housekeeping' which can be interpreted for each specific location.

The principle of ecological balance would have to be demonstrated on the developed land itself or in immediate functional integration with it. Many ecologically important interactions are sensitive, such as cold air streams, which are so important for the city climate and are obstructed even by minor obstacles. If this rule is combined with the principle of short distances to recreational landscape areas, then the number of high-density residential areas with fully sealed open spaces is set within strict limits.

If one wants to limit land available for development, one must first address the areas with employment land uses, because this is where the largest reserves of sites are available. However, there is vehement opposition to this from trade and industry. No city in Germany has so far been able to impose on its commercial and trade sectors the need for denser construction, or production and storage in multi-storey structures because the business community would move to adjacent municipalities, which do not impose such obligations. On the contrary, municipalities encourage an uneconomical use of land and sites through subsidising land prices in employment areas.

The land for transport infrastructure also comprises major land reserves that could be mobilised, if standards were not so strictly applied and the traffic departments were not so technocratically independent. On the other hand, most community facilities, such as schools and kindergartens, have a large requirement for open spaces and cannot be constructed with such an economical use of land. They could, however, be integrated into multi-storey structures and thus reduce the built-over surface area.

The call for higher density housing over and above a moderate level is, for the most part, an argument which benefits the pockets of individual land owners and builders, who stand to profit from it. On the other hand, denser development is more and more unavoidable and this makes it such a favourite of local authority politicians because the land for house building has to be bought at such a high price that it must be exploited to an irresponsibly high degree. This has the consequence that the responsibility for everything which should belong to the residential environment, from the car parking to recreational facilities, is shifted to the public areas. For example, streets are made into car parks and play areas are edged out into the public parks. The shortage of open space in turn intensifies the leisure traffic and puts a strain on other residential areas.

Another question is whether through high land prices and the general alteration of the standards for good quality dwellings, the residential area ratio which has grown exponentially can be reduced. For this purpose, supplementary functions – such as baths, community rooms, even kitchens formerly shared by several families – placed close to but outside the dwelling could make a contribution. However, such a change would have to make inroads into standards of comfort that are only one generation old and, perhaps precisely for that reason, so precious. Consequently this would have to be introduced over the long term. A personal room, a bathroom, a separate WC and a kitchen of one's own – these are attributes of the most recent generation, but have become taken for granted and no one will readily give them up.[34]

However, it must be repeated that the major reserves of land and floor space are in the employment rather than residential areas. My thesis is that for ecological improvements the stabilisation and reduction of the specific residential and employment land uses (per inhabitant/per employee) are more important than disproportionate development densities. What we need is the uncoupling of the evolution of prosperity and the consumption of land, in the same way as the uncoupling of productivity and the consumption of energy has already been achieved.

The presumption that the density of the city in the nineteenth century functioned so well is misleading. It could only be built so densely because the provision of communal services and facilities, especially of open space, was irresponsibly poor, but above all because there were no cars. Anyone who has had to bring up small children in such an otherwise attractive and urban quarter from the nineteenth century knows that, because the streets are much too dangerous, children have to rely on special fenced-off playgrounds which they can only safely reach when helped by adults.

Hong Kong and Singapore have development and social densities, which are far above those of the European city of the nineteenth century. However, they only function because the horizontal layering of uses is implemented consistently – with uses of low daylight requirement in the multiple-floor base zones and the residential high-rise flats above them, and also, because numerous open spaces have been established on the roofs of the base zones. The climate, in which shadow is more preferable than sun, helps this considerably.

In Asia the evolution of a new type of city can be observed, with its own strict rules and norms which have nothing to do with European traditions.[35] So far, this city type could only be implemented under non-democratic, authoritarian conditions, and it remains to be seen whether its power of attraction would also apply in societies with democratic administrations and governments.

However, the most important factor for the social acceptance of Hong Kong is that everywhere there exists a close visual and spatial connection with the landscape of the sea and the mountains. In the assessment of the phenomenal density of Hong Kong, sea and mountains must always be included. However, it must be repeated and emphasised that in the last few decades large residential areas with really high densities, even if they are not of the Hong Kong/Singapore type, have no longer been achievable in free and democratically governed societies, despite their ecological advantages.

Mixed use

Mention of Hong Kong brings us to the concept of mixed use. This is said to be a necessary component of urban-ness and an effective means to minimise motorised traffic. In principle this is acceptable, particularly because the increasing proportion of service employees promotes a mixture of residential and employment buildings. At the same time, however, a question must be raised about what type of mixture is meant: is it a mix in the building itself, in the interaction with the street or in the urban quarter?

The answer depends on what objective is to be achieved through the mix. If we want a small-scale balance of interests and the direct mutual responsibility from people living and working together with different incomes and different qualifications, then we will want the mixed use plot of land, in principle as small as possible, to form the building block of the city.[36] Only through a mixture of uses on the plot and in the fabric of the building itself will it be possible to integrate the various uses according to their relative sensitivities in terms of orientation, access, inflow of utilities and emissions in such a way that they can achieve maximum density, without restricting sensitive residential uses.

However, are the conditions for this type of small grain mixed use still created, apart from a small number of medium-sized providers? The mixed use plot of the nineteenth century in major cities such as Vienna, Berlin and Budapest was a structure optimised through economics and planning. Different locations had different qualities: the front building, carefully distinguished in rental terms between basement, *piano nobile*, upper floors and attic; in the back crafts workshops, storage premises and, last but not least, the back building for tenants of limited means. All were integrated with each other into a type of building complex which offered maximum utilisation of the land. At the same time, thanks to the distribution of risk, this type of building guaranteed a medium-scale capital investment as pension insurance, particularly since the broad range of different forms of capital investment, which are available today, did not exist. In addition, this mixed use plot resulted in a fine-grained social mixture, and this had great advantages as pointed out by James Hobrecht.[37]

Today, however, the socio-economic conditions for such a type of building are missing. The spatial requirements of the different types of use, which have become more specific since the nineteenth century, render a vertical mixture inside the building difficult. The criteria for residential quality are subject to high level statutory standards. Above all, however, the middle-class client for such mixed use buildings has become a rarity. His place is being taken by the major capital of the banks and insurance companies with their anonymous funds. The switch from direct material investment to relatively abstract forms of investment in shares, bank securities and funds is difficult to stop, although strenuous efforts should be made to link citizens, as owners of their own plot and building, with their city.[38] Perhaps it would be feasible to combine a small, intermediate form of local, limited property fund with local capital and local commitment.

However, it is in another dimension that the mixture of use in the building itself will become significant: the dimension of time. For the purpose of longevity and to save resources, buildings must in future be capable of adjustment to changing demands, for example, by changing from office to residential and back again to office. This presupposes less functionally specialised buildings so that good conditions can be created for a small-scale mix of uses. But keeping the building flexible for other uses also presupposes structural redundancy through higher ceilings, larger-span structures or space for expansion. Today, which investor continues to think in the long term and is prepared to invest in flexibility? The normal case these days is the separation of different uses in different buildings along a street. This also applies at the scale of the urban district. Uses which have large space requirements and generate a high traffic volume with harmful emissions can be located along main roads allowing undisturbed integration of living and working (a structure which Roland Rainer wanted to adopt as a principle for the development plan of the city of Vienna as early as the 1960s).

In practice, however, even such efforts towards a mixture of uses encounter major obstacles and this is caused by the 'norms' of our economy. In the course of rationalisation and special-isation, both in production and in trading, as well as in the enter-tainment industry, larger and larger units with fewer and fewer employees are set up. These units are replacing a large number of smaller shops, workshops and cinemas and are hard to integrate into a small-scale structure. This trend towards large size applies also to delivery vehicles: a large articulated lorry cannot manoeu-vre in a small residential street. Finally, leisure time at the weekend and during holidays is more rigidly organised in the 'arti-ficial worlds' of bigger and bigger leisure centres with their com-prehensive range of consumer services.[39]

This is one of the main reasons for the apparent bleakness of our new city districts. Leisure time is spent elsewhere, and the last surviving corner shops in the beloved city quarters of the nineteenth century are expensive and will remain so because of a lack of opportunities for rationalisation. If we want to get away from the mono-functional tedium of our urban expansion we must do something to change this rationalisation and special-isation which appears to be forced on us by competition. Is this possible? There do seem to be some initial trends in retailing towards restoring neighbourhood shops. Perhaps a change in the opening hours of retail outlets will lead to the establishment, close to residential areas, of large kiosks which stay open until late at night and also take over other social communication tasks, as do the 'Büdchen' in Cologne. Such trends can be observed, for instance, in Scotland where the deregulation of the opening hours for shops has resulted in small and middle-sized outlets (shops, cafés, etc.) remaining open long hours, some even for 24 hours. Many shops, even large stores in the city centre, are also open all day Saturday and all Sunday afternoon. However, there are also trends in the other direction. Tele-shopping, for example, could potentially curb traditional retailing at the same time as increasing commercial traffic. But even without tele-shopping, in the day-to-day planning of new settlements, major supermarket chains see to it that, through contracts with the land owners, none of their com-petitors are allowed in.

Another important objective is a reduction of motorised traffic, which is sought through the maximum concentration of a wide mixture of uses. A dense integration of residential, employment and supply premises could substantially reduce the use of the car, promote pedestrians and cycling and at the same time contribute to a lively street life with natural, unobtrusive social control.

However, this very attractive line of argument is supported only by a small group of citizens who can still live in a unity of time, place and work For the majority the possibility of being able to choose a house and employment in spatial proximity has gone. This is due to the highly specialised and differentiated nature of society in time and space. Even within the family, daily routines are tending to drift away from each other. In addition, the residential wishes of all those on higher incomes are aimed directly at having a large amount of space, garden and proximity to the country, whereas their highly specialised and therefore highly paid jobs are frequently in large centrally located organisations. Today, instead of mixture we have an extreme spatial polarisation. The divisive effect of shorter working hours has already been referred to.

Nevertheless, everything suggests that the widest possible mixture in cities should be aimed for. Ever more extensive service uses can be well combined with residential uses. The trend to more and more living area per inhabitant will perhaps one day reverse in favour of the separation of specific functions from the dwelling and, like in Japan, their concentration in larger and relatively luxurious public facilities such as baths, hobby workshops and club premises. Admittedly, at the moment it does not look like this, but it is likely that one day declining purchasing power will force us once again to live more closely together. In the poor districts of our cities this reversal has already started. Telecommunications will not only promote such a development of decentralisation in the form of working from home but will also assist the decentralisation of offices.[40] In addition, such mixed use quarters of cities are simply more interesting. Mixed city quarters offer a specific part of the population the possibility of reaching their work and local facilities on foot or by bicycle. They offer children and adults a wider range of experiences and the less well-educated and less productive can find more opportunities for part-time work and informal occupation. Thus such urban areas are better suited to integrate the unemployed and immigrants.

Comparative studies of two urban areas in Frankfurt am Main were conducted in 1993. Each had an approximately equal proportion of immigrants, about 60 per cent, one was a well-developed and mixed inner-city district and the other a mono-functional peripheral estate planned and built in the 1960s. The studies show that the proportion of recipients of social security among immigrants in the inner-city quarter is about a third lower than in the peripheral estate.[41]

Mixed use districts will also offer better spatial conditions for new forms of neighbourhood help, by taking over social services that can no longer be provided on an economically viable basis by the public sector. The current highly concentrated social service systems are cost-intensive and have an alienating effect; therefore they need to be decentralised.[42] Finally, such districts provide a framework for ecologically determined energy and materials initiatives in which excessive waste energy or waste materials can be reprocessed locally. Therefore, mixed use districts are better equipped for difficult times.

However, the implementation of the ideal of a stronger mixture of uses is opposed, not only by rationalisation, specialisation and the economies of scale of production and retailing but also by an almost unrestrained real estate market. The highly differentiated markets, which have arisen in the course of the spatial and functional division of labour, exclude economically weaker uses. As a result, a mix of offices and flats in prime central locations has become very difficult to achieve.

Functional segregation is frequently regarded as the consequence of the Charter of Athens. This is largely nonsense. Functional segregation is the consequence of the differentiation of land values, which leads to an assortment of uses on the basis of their economic performance capacity and of the mutual disturbance tolerances of similar uses that permit the establishment of areas of like commercial and industrial uses with higher tolerance levels and the corresponding reduction of production costs.[43] Conversely, this leads to determining exceptionally low levels of permissible disturbance in new residential areas. The Charter of Athens, looked at in these terms, has done nothing more than elevate socio-economic 'norms' into ideological objectives, but in so doing has undoubtedly contributed to a confirmation of those very standards. Accordingly, the implementation of a functional mix presupposes at least the following: restricted sizes of enterprises which permit mixture of uses; a better control of noise, smells and traffic annoyance caused by the use itself, in order to render the principle of mutual disturbance tolerance superfluous; more or less equitable location in order to limit the price gap between land in different locations; and, not least, a greater tolerance towards the day-to-day disturbances of normal city life – in contrast to the present tendency which shows a decreasing tolerance with regard to noise from children's games and sport (accompanied by an astonishingly higher tolerance level of traffic noise).

The mixture of residential, commercial and services, so enjoyable although endangered in the centres of cities such as Berlin, Vienna, Barcelona and Budapest is essentially attributable to the balanced density and spatial structure of the nineteenth-century city over very large areas. This structure moderated the price of land and smoothed out price fluctuations because it supplied a broad spectrum of similar conditions at all locations. It is this quality, which expresses itself among other things in the typically consistent eaves heights, that is wantonly being discarded in Berlin, for example.

Ecology

With the arguments for reducing traffic, the energy crisis and material recycling, we reach our last and most difficult concept, that of 'urban ecology'. If at present there is one undisputed objective of city development, it is of the objective of 'sustainable city development', meaning the most compatible integration of the city into the natural cycle. Ecology has rightly become the overriding principle of city development. The ecosystem of the world would collapse if the type of urban development used in the industrialised world was carried out throughout the globe. For this reason, there is an urgent need to redirect this development.

The cities in old Europe have a good basis for doing this: they are relatively wealthy and their populations are more or less stable; agricultural land has to be reduced as a result of overproduction; and the average level of education is high. European cities could in fact show the world how to make cities sustainable, before environmental catastrophes force us to do so.[44] However, what approach should be selected and to what end?

This question can be broken down into two opposing theses:

1   The city must necessarily, by its very essence, stand opposed to nature.
2   The city can be a component of a man-made nature.

These two theses are based on fundamentally different concepts of the city and of nature. The first thesis supposes that man and the city are outside nature, indeed against nature, and cause profound damage to the natural basis of life. According to this view, human beings should emancipate themselves from the arbitrary regularities of nature. They should control the circulation of materials in closed cycles, use as little area as possible for settlement confined to the most ecological insensitive locations and restrict their interactions with nature to an unavoidable minimum. Their systems should have as few links to nature as possible so that nature is left to itself.

This approach, granting nature a status of its own as orthodox environmental protection asserts, is in contrast to the idea that interprets man and the city as a particular part of nature, which would, even in the parts which merit protection, not exist without man. The city has, for a long time, become a 'second nature', with a diversity of plant and animal life which exceeds the richness of the surrounding agrarian landscape. The larger the city, the greater is its natural diversity.[45] But human beings must understand that, as biological creatures, they must stop destroying their bases of life which they have been artificially cultivating over centuries.

Yet, the distinction between 'original' nature and 'technically manipulated' nature becomes more and more difficult. In the city and its environs nature meets the human being predominantly in technically modified and influenced forms. Furthermore, human beings no longer directly experience the conditions of nature which are important for their well-being. This happens in an intermediate way through abstract data-measurement – such as air pollution, the ozone content of the atmosphere, the nitrate content of groundwater, and the presence of heavy metals in the ground – which, nevertheless, profoundly characterise their mental image of nature. There is no longer any escape from this inter-permeation of nature and human technology.[46]

In the exaggerated forms outlined above, both basic theses are unproductive for our discussion of the city, and any approach which is to be useful for day-to-day practice must look for a position that mediates between these two extremes. I personally incline more towards the latter view, of a nature made human, and would like to look a little more at its consequences.

A glance at the aerial photograph of any of our major conurbations shows that the area settlement relationship between city and countryside has been reversed. The open countryside has become an internal figure against the 'background' of the settled area. The settled area itself could be interpreted as a special form of 'landscape', which contains the open land. Both areas, the internal landscape free of development and the settlement itself are nearly completely man-made. One can justifiably claim that, at least in the environment of the city, everything – city and open space – is built. We may criticise this or regret it, but we cannot escape from it.

If one pursues this line of thought a little further against the background of the historical development of our culture, then the ecological and cultural continuum of a built structure exists between the countryside and the city. This continuous *cultura*, in the original Latin meaning of the cultivated and constructed, presents itself, for example, as an agriculturally and economically effective field, greenhouse culture, allotments, the old single-family housing estate on large plots of land, a settlement colony, the city quarter of the nineteenth century and also as a high-rise quarter with roof gardens. Each of the structural elements, and not only the areas free of buildings, must make their contribution as *cultura* in preserving both our socio-economic and our natural basis of life. This would presuppose a radical change to the meaning of construction. Buildings could, for example, be interpreted as 'artificial rock formations', which can shelter specific plants and animals. The cultural and natural inheritance of a plot of land would have to be protected and developed in tandem with each other. 'Accordingly "building" should not be assessed as an intervention in nature but should be understood as a seed of change, which in the long term will lead to new spaces and areas which merit protection.'[47]

We would then take seriously the fact that we ourselves are, in the profoundest sense, responsible for the bases of our life. We would then understand that we cannot obtain absolution through compensation measures, through an appeal to good Mother

Nature and her ability to cope with our demands, and that we cannot redeem ourselves with penance payments for acts of previous indulgence thereby avoiding the question of what nature we actually want for ourselves.

In many cases the 'the rules governing intervention and compensation' illustrate absurd tendencies. Some environmental protection authorities seem to be more interested in securing high compensation payments in return for the approval of damaging building interventions in order to be able to 'construct' biotopes in another place.

In any case, these rules deal much too briefly with the ecological burden as the concept of 'the ecological footprint' shows. The ecological impact of cities with regard to importing raw materials and exporting waste stretches far beyond the immediate environment to different countries and continents. Here, any rules are not much more than a sedative, intended to produce a clear conscience. What is needed is a more comprehensive, radical perspective and another concept of cultural landscape.

The history of the cultural landscape shows that it has been constantly changing and that the type of cultural landscape which is used as a yardstick today for the protection of culture and landscape originates in the late nineteenth and early twentieth century and necessarily possesses the traits of the transitional state of this period.[48]

Today particularly popular landscapes are the result of large and forcible interventions. As an example, we might mention the heaths and moorlands which were understood as the quintessence of the cultural landscape and which today are understood to be worthy of protection. They are the result of a systematic destruction of woodland and a ruinous exploitation of the land. Nevertheless, their preservation is regarded as a task of nature conservancy. This involves the retention of the cultural landscape of earlier centuries, and at the same time the preservation of the coevolution of the cultural landscape and its fauna and flora. Even large landscapes and parks – which in cultural terms today are so significant and deserving of natural protection, for instance that in Muskau, a famous park in East Germany, created in the first half of the nineteenth century – are the result of an almost complete alteration of a pre-existing situation. It was the great landscape

architect Prince Pückler-Muskau who completely converted
the existing landscape and was criticised for this intervention.
He 'punished' himself by granting the citizens a new town hall
as a 'compensation'. But precisely the interventions which
occurred at that time are now the eminently important park
landscapes in and around Muskau worthy of cultural and
natural protection.

In the spirit of this dynamic evolution, the objective should
be developing new types of cultural landscape in which the production of foodstuffs, ecological equilibrium and recreation are
brought into a new synthesis. A comparable conclusion also
applies to building. The contrast between built-up areas and the
countryside must also be overcome in this new synthesis.[49]

Finally on this subject, another recommendation from ecosystem
research suggests that:

> Cities must again become more strongly integrated into the
> surrounding landscape. The procurement of drinking water
> should in the medium term be redirected from the utilisation
> of groundwater to the use of surface water with its lower
> degree of wastage. The exploitation of waste water should,
> after the separation or separate purification of industrial waste
> water, be similar to that in rural settlement areas. In order to
> reduce the heat absorption of the city, as large as possible an
> amount of vegetation should be planted on roofs, façades and
> around buildings and rainwater should not be drained away
> but used for cultivation. Finally, the production of foodstuffs
> should again take place close to the city in order to minimise
> expensive transport costs. Some of the foodstuffs could be
> produced on the periphery of the city in greenhouses. An
> attempt could also be made through artificial food chains to
> convert biomass not reusable as foodstuffs e.g. algae into food
> for humans e.g. fish.[50]

We cannot avoid the need to compose our thoughts about the cultural landscape suited to our society, because it will have to be different from the old cultural landscape for which we are so
nostalgic. This cultural landscape will be an urbanised landscape
in the urban regions, a landscape between culture and nature.[51]

The city of tomorrow will consist of a concentration of compact settlements surrounded and surrounding countryside, which meets specific city functions. Open land as an internal structure of the city has the potential for water and material cycles. These new, functional perspectives have retroactive effects on commercial and residential structures, on the profile of the landscape and the aspect of recreation. The identity of the city is derived not only from the design and mode of functioning of the built-up area, but also from the undeveloped open, 'vegetative' areas.'[52]

City and countryside will have to be involved in a new symbiosis, polarised between biotechnical systems in the city and new wildernesses in the countryside. City ecology will change from a science which is used predominantly for the analysis and protection of the remaining landscape into a discipline which actively develops new forms of urban and cultural landscapes.

Periphery

City peripheries are often used only as functional space. They contain DIY warehouses, suburbs, dormitories and leisure centres. Significant places are found elsewhere: historic city centres, entertainment and recreational areas, and tourist destinations. For two years, I have been conducting tours for local people and visitors through the expanse of the periphery of the city of Cologne. On these two-day excursions, I attempt to give a feeling for the beauty of this discontinuous area characterised over great stretches by the absence of what can be perceived as an event. The discontinuity of Cologne's periphery, particularly on the 'Schäl Sick' (bad side of Cologne) which is regularly dissected by motorways and railways, enables spatial sequences which are particularly rich in surprises. The recreational quality of 'empty' places on the one hand and the fractal richness and diversity of the newly arising forms of life which sustain themselves in the shadow of the competition between metropolises on the other hand are the special characteristics of this city edge. As a result of the continuous status of the city of Cologne as a citadel, lasting from Roman antiquity to the end of the First World War, and later through its role as a traffic interchange of West Germany, the gaps in the city profile are particularly numerous and form a decisive design feature at all scales.

Viewed from the centre

What would New York be without Brooklyn and Queens, Paris without its banlieues, a harbour city without the ocean, Cairo without the desert? Only in contact with wilderness do we recognise the conditions of culture. Indeed, civilised life is not possible without this knowledge of the conditions of culture.

This mode of reading the periphery as a wilderness is the counterpoint to the mode of reading the periphery as countryside. Both readings are justified, as an aid to interpretation and through the specific experience of the city's peripheral areas.

- The periphery is a complex cultural landscape where individual, unacquired areas without preconceived form, such as undeveloped land and car parks, form wildernesses.
- The periphery is a no-man's land, a macrostructure without preconceived form or forethought, in which numerous individually designed and acquired microstructures are distributed.

Consuming and productive perception

The capacity to decipher impressions, i.e. 'raw' information, to make it able to be imaged and to interpret it, and the capacity to fill gaps through one's associations, memories and projections, I call this productive and sentimental perception.

Since we come from the world of deciphered information, we begin to feel boredom in the anonymous, inconspicuous, uncultivated places. What we find we cannot read leads to boredom then irritation. Only after some time does productive perception come into effect, and the world around us begins to fill up. Empty spaces are necessary in order to develop the capacities which make man into a cultural being: opening up, adding, interpreting, associating, projecting and remembering.

Aesthetic sustainability

What is experienced negatively as fragmentation and incoherence through the inability to perceive the whole can also be perceived as a high degree of complexity through richness in discontinuities, richness in ecological and social niches and as a subjective spatial enlargement. In the long term, meaningful surroundings will never form single images. Each viewing should create new, vague and ill-defined glimmers of images.

Prominence and anywhere

A prominent place always has an easily perceivable image for its structure, usually a geometric one.

Without a connection to somewhere the prominent place becomes a mere tourist attraction. Without the anonymous the renowned becomes a cliché.

Bilderstöckchen, a neighbourhood at the northern edge of Cologne

Group of urban tourists on a waste deposit in the east of Cologne

Weidenpesch, a neighbourhood at the northern edge of Cologne

Small wood in Poll

Chapter 2

An interpretation of the *Zwischenstadt*

As I tried to show in the first chapter, the city is changing into something new, which we perceive and evaluate differently depending on our previous experience and personal attitudes. Given that for the past twenty or so years the benchmark was the idealised Old City, our attitude to the *Zwischenstadt* is undergoing a radical change. After a period of the principal condemnation of the 'cancerous growth of city and the ensuing consumption of the countryside', now – following Venturi's *Learning from Las Vegas* and clinging to a rather fashionable obsession with Tokyo – in a certain 'school' of architects and town planners the pendulum of judgement has to some extent started to swing towards an uncritical obsession with the 'fractal richness' and the 'anarchic dynamic' of the *Zwischenstadt*. I want to avoid both perspectives, by tracing the potential of the *Zwischenstadt* and confronting the disintegrated city with its still intensifying social and cultural problems which are part of its structural attributes. The chapter will conclude by setting out propositions on the significance of the intelligibility and legibility of the *Zwischenstadt*.

Perspectives and questions

This chapter attempts to provide a clear description of the *Zwischenstadt* and its causes, to disenchant the myth of the Old City, and to provide a critical analysis of the main essential terminology. The intention is to assist in seeing the reality of our cities no less critically, but rather in a less prejudiced way. In particular, we can see that the open countryside is changing from being the background of the city to being a figure bordered by the mass of settlement; we can see that the city cores are acquiring the character of shopping centres, and that the shopping malls of the *Zwischenstadt* are seeking to match the city centre in urban-ness; we can see that the cities' historical cores only constitute a small fraction of the city and that other centres of attraction have emerged on the periphery.

If we attempt to take an unbiased look at this cluster of different city areas, we can perceive the *Zwischenstadt* in a sympathetic manner as a unique 'city archipelago' with its own qualities.

Instead of talking dismissively about urban sprawl, we could recognise that there is a fine-grained interpenetration of open space and built form and see the open space as the binding element, with its new creative potential. Instead of criticising the lack of urban-ness, we could perceive a decentralised cultural diversity, with new possibilities for cultural activities. These new activities would certainly be different from the culture of the Old City but none the worse for that, because they reach more people. Instead of complaining about the loss of centrality, we could recognise a modern network structure and thus the emergence of a new model of order more akin to our pluralistic and democratic society than the old model of centres.

A judgement which is free of prejudice is also required because the real possibilities for change are limited. Not only the city cores are almost complete in their structural form, but the *Zwischenstadt* is also essentially fully developed and a reality, and the need for new buildings should be relatively modest if we are to make better use of the existing building stock.

This could, however, lead to the mistaken conclusion that we would have to make do with the city as we find it. The opposite is the case. Never before in history has the city as a cultural product been so malleable as it is today. The conditions for the location of most functions have relaxed to such an extent that in principle they can be combined in a much freer way than before. This is not just because of telecommunications, but also because, thanks to reduced working hours and jobs in services and telecommunications, people are at least in some areas much freer than before in their dealings with space and time and can therefore develop completely different life styles. Accordingly, employment and the disposition of work can, at least in part, be spatially and temporally relaxed.

To say that the scope for designing the city is considerable sounds at first rather paradoxical in view of the fact that the basic structure of cities is effectively unalterable and that the conduct of human beings can hardly be influenced by the tools available to spatial planning. However, the paradox is resolved if we add the dimension of time. Essentially what we need is to exploit the necessary and therefore continuous changes of use, conversions, repairs, renovations, adjustments, displacements and processes of the modernisation of the city which, depending on the space or sector under consideration, constitute an average rate of change of about 2–5 per cent a year. Within one generation, a city can be substantially remodelled by small-scale changes, if the innumerable individual measures are orientated towards and co-ordinated by a few major overriding social objectives.[53]

There are major opportunities for transformation in the reform of agriculture as a result of ecological and agrarian necessities. The scale of the reorganisation of agriculture makes it an issue for political decisions at the level of the EC. Farmers already obtain about half of their income from general tax funds and, through the policy of the European Community, they are restricted in their commercial freedom to such an extent that they are practically told what they can grow and how much of their land they have to leave fallow. Why should this area of policy not be more integrated with town planning? Why not, at last, develop a new countryside integrated with the *Zwischenstadt* and a new cultural landscape in which the production of food, recreation and ecological balance forms a new unity between built-up and open areas?[54] That would make sense in order to process and develop the hidden advantages of the *Zwischenstadt* and in stages to mitigate the disadvantages. Both these procedures are described by Karl Ganser as follows:

> The advantages which are so often overlooked are smallness of scale, mixture of functions, polycentric structure instead of 'excessive centralisation', oriented towards one dominating city centre. Criticism is directed at the 'settlement pulp', the lack of separation between settlement and countryside, the car dependent settlement form, the lack of clarity and alleged lack of urban-ness.[55]

Economic and functional objectives should not be pushed into the foreground to such an extent in the design of the *Zwischenstadt*. These can be achieved these days with almost any form of city. Cultural and ecological objectives should be in the foreground because the view of the city as a cultural product and the view of the open areas as a new cultural landscape are not only theoretically significant. In the future cultural and ecological qualities will become a decisive commercial factor because 'hard' infrastructures, for example, good road connections or high-performance cable networks, will be available more or less everywhere. This will mean that unique place-specific and not easily reproducible qualities and properties, such as cultural richness and beauty of landscape, will be the most important conditions for development, because they will become significant economic attractions.

In such an interpretation of the *Zwischenstadt*, some central questions are raised:

1 How will time be dealt with in the *Zwischenstadt*? The protection of historic monuments and, where appropriate, that of the building stock is important and indispensable in order to retain the historical and temporal depth of the city. But how are we to leave room for the future? How are we going to reserve space for manoeuvre so that the *Zwischenstadt* can renew and adjust itself in a consistent cyclic economy without constant small- and large-scale demolition? Who will pay for and secure this room for manoeuvre? What will the path look like that leads us from the original value of individual buildings, through the period of their disuse and apparent uselessness, to the restoration of their value? What is the importance of fallow land in the cycle of development as 'breathing space' for nature and as cultural and commercial 'room for manoeuvre' for people?[56]

2 What are we to do about nature in the future? The protection of nature is essential in order to retain the 'historical' nature as an object of living experience in the city. However, is the ideal image of the pre-industrial cultural landscape still adequate as a benchmark? Should not take a much more radical approach? With the help of a creatively understood 'development ecology', we could abolish the old contrast between the badness of nature-destroying development and

the goodness of healing Mother Nature in order to generate new forms of landscape. Hopefully, later generations will one day love and protect them just as we today protect our old cultural landscapes.[57] Should it not be our aim to find and develop a new symbiosis between developed areas and the cultural landscape?

3   How are we to deal with the diversity of lifestyles and cultures? Cultural plurality is a positive characteristic of the *Zwischenstadt*, but how are we to make sure that an entity, which is becoming more and more dispersed and multi-centred and is fostering more and more differentiated lifestyles, does not disintegrate into jealously guarded districts with different income levels and lifestyles? Will the residential appeal of the qualitatively differentiated locations in the *Zwischenstadt* remain so balanced that socio-economic differences stay within manageable limits? Can the network of public spaces, streets and squares, parks and lakes, landscapes and rivers be formed in such a way that the average citizens become curious about the diversity of the *Zwischenstadt*? So that they will want to discover its tensions and contrasts between public and secret, order and chaos, high culture and garden gnome, between districts bursting with dynamism and those which seem to have been asleep from time immemorial, between accepted beauty and the discovery of beauty in the ugly? Can the *Zwischenstadt* in its functional, socio-economic and cultural differentiation be made readable and liveable as a homogeneous community?[58]

These three questions about the essence of time and development, nature and culture, differentiation and living together are directed at the identity of the *Zwischenstadt*. Is it more than an intellectual construct? Can it be experienced as an integrated living space, as something which can be perceived through the senses? Karl Ganser comments on the *Zwischenstadt* of the Ruhr area: 'It is necessary to create orientation and draft images which render this encoded landscape legible. This could facilitate the development of a new understanding of regional planning.'

In other words, can concealed connections be rendered visible and linked with each other in such a way that in the minds of citizens mental images are created which render the city region usable without the need for maps and posters? Could these images also encapsulate the broad cultural resource of the *Zwischenstadt* as well as particular offers of employment and interesting leisure destinations? Could it become the objective of a new type of planning and part of metropolitan culture to make the 'cosmos' of one's own city legible with the help of suitable 'constellation' patterns? Could we record the unique 'music' of the metropolis in a 'score' and develop visions which open up the *Zwischenstadt* as a sphere of experience?

The cultural and political dissolution of the city

Before attempting to answer these questions, the social and political status of the *Zwischenstadt* must be discussed because, without this basis, all attempts to make the *Zwischenstadt* available as a space for living and experience would be futile. We need good political and social reasons for endeavouring to achieve this objective, because the process of rendering the *Zwischenstadt* legible and imageable requires a leap of faith and the combination of several areas of policy (town planning and agriculture, culture and sport, traffic and the economy readily spring to mind). Then again this would only be desirable if we were interested in something more than just good orientation and aesthetic experiences. The great political effort required would only make sense if it could lead to a contribution being made to a new agreement between *Zwischenstadt* and society. This is an ambitious objective. The French sociologist Alain Touraine recently denied that we still had a 'city' or 'society' in the old sense: 'It is neither good nor bad, it just is as it is.'[59] Although coming from a quite different starting point, this line of thought fits in with my own and will, therefore, be quoted and commented on in detail in what follows. According to Touraine:

> The social and technical environment in which we live has destroyed the city as a political institution in a more radical way than industrial society. If we had to combine the social characteristics of today's world into a single thought, I would say without hesitation that its most important characteristic is the separation, the division, the drifting apart of the two sides

of the human experience: on the one hand, we have the world of exchange, which is globalised and is consequently de-socialised. On the other hand – as a direct consequence and reaction against this – we have the replacement of social and political man with private man.

Touraine then raises the question of whether this should be accepted or whether policy should set itself against this development; and talking of 'the breaking apart and the scattered elements' he addresses both the spatial problems of the *Zwischenstadt* and also the social problems of a society which is disintegrating into brashly competing individuals, a society that has not yet mastered the transition from 'you' through 'I' to 'we':

> The question is – a question which I might call a 'political' question in the noblest sense of the word – whether we accept this breaking apart of cities and societies or whether we think that we can put the scattered elements back together into a kind of unity. This is the question which arises, and this is the most difficult, apparently almost insoluble question which we are confronted with.

However, at the same time, he warns against a regression into pseudo-historical forms and in so doing underlines the danger that the myth of the historical city will obstruct our view:

> In fact, as soon as I raise this question, it is apparent that certain things are impossible. Going back, re-establishing Polis-cities, returning priority to politics – all this appears to us as artificial. Artificial, because of the internationalisation of the economy, because of the restoration of identities [of the 'private man', Thomas Sieverts], which I have discussed. I say this all the more clearly because the subject of the rebuilding of cities, the reintegration of cities, is an extremely popular subject and in my opinion one of the most reactionary topics of contemporary life.

And thus he comes to the decisive problem which we are confronted with regarding the formation of the *Zwischenstadt*, and he agrees with the definition of the problem offered by André Gorz, as developed in his *Critique of Economic Reason*.[60] It is the problem of combining work, which is necessarily alienated in the global division of labour, with a meaningful life:

> Now, I have rejected this fraudulent solution, this type of neo-urban or neo-medieval city ideology, we must reflect on the solutions which one can actually find. The problem therefore consists not just in finding out how we can facilitate the cohabitation of different people but in finding out how one can combine this openness, this internationalisation, this speed with which technology and other things are developing in specific areas with the diversity and the increasingly limited reactions oriented towards identity or community.

Like André Gorz, Alain Touraine sees the connection of globalisation with a fulfilled life not in the collective, but in the experience and development of each person's individual life:

> I believe that one has to say very clearly that the link between the public world of the economy and the fractured and closed world of cultural identities can only be achieved at the level of the experiences of individual life. By this I mean that each individual, regardless who it is, you and I, the great technical expert or the unemployed labourer, has to live simultaneously in a world of technology and the market and with an inheritance, a memory, a language, a very definite cultural tradition.

In the further course of his argument, Alan Touraine deals with the extreme fragmentation and individualisation of living spaces as we typically find them in the *Zwischenstadt*:

> I believe that the solutions which we must look for are solutions which will be set at the lowest possible level, and by this I mean solutions which will be concentrated as little as possible on restoring cities and based as strongly as possible, and as far as possible, on allowing the largest possible number of people to be here and somewhere else at the same time.

In this connection he argues in favour of accepting the fragile, incomplete and transitory dimension which is so typical of the

Zwischenstadt and which leaves scope for experience and appropriation:

> Because the city is a complex system, it must also be treated as such, i.e. as something with many 'loopholes', gaps, open spaces, spaces for adjustment and change. It is necessary to create at the level of lived experience, of life experience, the fundamental experiences of the individual, a relationship between participation in the world of technology and economy on the one hand and participation in a cultural identity on the other.

Alain Touraine emphasises the significance of the individual for this establishment of a connection between the world of the division of labour in the economy and participation in the personal wealth of the family and the group, but does this not put an excessive challenge on the individual? Do we not also need other supporting 'intermediary' institutions? This is a challenge to local authority policy on which Touraine also has important things to say. It is likely that the political conclusions which he draws from his line of argument, namely the strange inversion of right and left in politics, will be the most important ones for our handling of the *Zwischenstadt*.

He feels himself obliged

> to examine this remarkable reversal of ideologies which we are observing in a more general context. What is normally known as 'the left' had traditionally a positive attitude towards the collective and the universal. What is known as 'the right' in general has been equated with the defence of particular historical and cultural interests. Today, in my opinion, the fronts on the political battlefield have been completely turned round. What one might call 'the right' is characterised by giving priority to international markets, non-social and non-political adjustment mechanisms. On the other hand, what is known as 'the left' is concentrating on the question of how the identities of communities and their individual and collective projects can be combined with this openness to the world. In other words, what is known as 'the left' is forced to apportion an increasing significance to subjective things, to memory, to tradition, to cultural diversity.

This means that in the planning of the *Zwischenstadt* the pursuit of primarily cultural and ecological, not economic objectives, can be presented as a genuine position of the left which can be understood as being in touch with the tradition of left-wing politics.

> It is certain that from now on and in the next decades the local problems, these, as we might say, 'urban problems' will be in the centre of the great debates and the great social and political conflicts. We must decide whether we want to revive the urban, social and political efforts to mediate between communities and a world market or whether we want to accept this increasing separation.

Touraine goes on to say:

> I think that there is continuity in the thinking of the left if it sets itself the primary objective of preventing the disintegration and the complete destruction of our city. At the same time it must endeavour to find ways and means to integrate the personal and collective identity with participation in the world of markets and of technology at the level of personal experience, at the level of the small, local units in the city districts and finally at the level of the region.

These sociological conditions and political positions, proposed by Alain Touraine at the meeting of the 'Social Democratic Association for Local Authority Policy' in the autumn of 1995, provide support for the seven theses which will be put forward in the following discussion. What Touraine has said about the political decision levels will also be valid:

> What has already been said almost jokingly about the nation state could also be said about the city. It is too big for the little problems and too small for the big problems. What sounds like a joke is in reality a dramatic observation which, one might add, points to the scale of the state [in our context the region] for the resolution of major problems and to the scale of the urban district for those of minor problems.

Theses on the significance of the intelligibility of the *Zwischenstadt*

It is against this social and political background that the following seven theses for making the *Zwischenstadt* intelligible, legible and thus imageable are to be understood. The objective is to mediate between the clarity of the familiar personal environment for living and working and the complexity of the city region. This regional level is perhaps a comprehensible intermediary between the perceptible place of residence and the abstract world market, a level at which a certain reconciliation between city and society can still be achieved.

1   The city regions are on the way to growing together into a more or less uniform and continuous living area. Social ties transcend the individual cities and form an integrated employment and leisure market, the vitality and availability of which will be one of the key factors in inter-regional competition. In order to be fully able to exploit the mutually complementary advantages of the spatial and functional division of labour in the region, the separately developed locational qualities of the diverse parts of the urban region need to be combined to a mutually complementary whole. At present, each local unit in the region is still seeking to offer more or less the same thing. The advantage of being a component of a city region with spatial and functional divisions, within which local identities are brought into play as strengths, are not yet really perceived, because we do not have an internal image of the city region.

2   The consciousness of being an inhabitant of a holistic city region will gain in significance with the changes which are already perceivable today in lifestyles. The old family structures, which provide support and security, are dissolving. More and more people have no children to look after them when they are old. We need new social ties and homes for people who have to live in uncertain circumstances. Traditional patterns of life are evolving into separate careers for different stages of life with multiple changes of lifestyle and environments – 'the flexible lifestyle'.[61] Old professional profiles are disappearing. Lifelong professional mobility is required through the utilisation of

market niches and opportunities provided by an employment market that is spread widely. Only a large regional employment market can offer such benefits. Incomes will tend to stagnate, in some circumstances even to fall, but the working time needed to achieve the required financial income will further diminish, although it will be unequally distributed over the lifetime. Having several different jobs simultaneously will not be an exception. Many inhabitants of the region will be at least temporarily unemployed and will then have to retrain. This will mean that specialised and differentiated educational and cultural opportunities will be essential to allow life to blossom in the region.

3 The blossoming of life in these altered socio-economic conditions will include a new relationship to 'place' that strengthens identity and provides support. When the orientation of life to a meaningful and well-planned professional for life is undermined for economic reasons and most employment is established in an alienating, globalised context, other anchors need to be formed that provide socio-cultural support. One such anchor could be the home location in the *Zwischenstadt*, if it enables lively political, social and cultural participation and real perceptual experiences. The over-structuring of perception by the electronic media, in particular television as the 'window on the world', and the consequent loss of the perception of reality must be counteracted by actual perceptual experience and the practical social as well as political potential for the formation of actual space.[62]

4 Increasing ecological problems, particularly in areas such as the disposal of refuse and waste water, energy production and transport, require urgent regional cooperation. Cooperation will, however, not be politically achievable on the required scale if the region is perceived only in an abstract mode, through statistical indicators and technical infrastructure networks, or through specialist groupings, for instance, for waste water and rubbish disposal. While they are very important, they tend to have rather negative connotations. Effective cooperation can only be achieved if the city region is imageable, i.e. can be perceived as a living space, can be experienced with the senses and, most of all, is coupled with positive images and experiences.[63]

5 Despite growing functional interconnections, city regions run the risk of disintegrating in political, social and cultural terms into a series of selfish and competitive urban fragments made up of different income groups and lifestyles, in particular, if the resources for compensation payments are reduced, or do not exist at all as in the UK and if socio-economic disparities combine with large-scale spatial segregation. This development can be observed in the USA, where many local communities have already begun to fence themselves off and bunker themselves in against socio-economically weaker groups and the public space between them has become a precarious no-man's land. The tendency in the USA is that in a few decades the proportion of the population in such 'gated' communities and ghettos will rise from 12 per cent to approximately 30 per cent. These are communities which no longer need to use any communal services, therefore do not pay any local taxes and which exclude themselves from the city community.[64] This development, which can be observed in its initial phase in Europe, must not be accepted.

6 A city region can only develop its total potential richness of concealed charms, commercial activities, lifestyles, environments and cultural opportunities, and thus have the potential for attracting and sustaining a large population, if it is made accessible from outside through good traffic networks. But it must also be internally accessible so that distances are thought of in terms of minutes and that the relevant special local qualities, which leave their own distinct impressions upon the memory, can be combined into a more or less direct and fixed network of images. This will mean that, in the course of the more intensive utilisation of space in the region, the initial rudimentary outline sketch will change and become enriched with details and colours.

7 Consequently, a feeling of belonging together must be promoted, so much so that a lively awareness arises that the city region is more than a sum of technical or specialist administrative unions and jealously competing districts. Such an awareness cannot be produced theoretically. It can only grow with a sense of pride in the region as one's home and an associated curiosity regarding the long-term 'exploration' of the region. In other words, interest in one's home area and

incentives for an inner regional 'tourism' must be developed. However, the feeling of belonging together will only develop and take shape if there is a politically independent, democratically legitimated, regional administration.

For these reasons, intensive efforts to improve the legibility and intelligibility of the *Zwischenstadt* seem to be more than merely a nice cultural addition. Indeed, legibility and intelligibility are the preconditions for perceiving and experiencing the city region as a space which shapes everyday life. Legibility and intelligibility are two of the most important conditions for the difficult task of regenerating an identity of society and space for everyday life in the *Zwischenstadt*.

Gelsenkirchen Bismarck

The historic maps show the process of development of an industrially characterised *Zwischenstadt*. Until late into the nineteenth century, there was a poor agrarian economy with individual, evenly distributed farmhouses but without real villages. In the last third of the nineteenth century, major railway systems developed and workers' colonies arose along the old roads as a result of coal mining. Before 1900, the first schools and churches, graveyards and religious social facilities followed. In the following decades, further workers colonies were built along with sports centres and allotments and other industries connected with mining, until the land was almost fully occupied. For several years, industrial development has been in recession, mining has ceased and the disused sites are offering new opportunities for development.

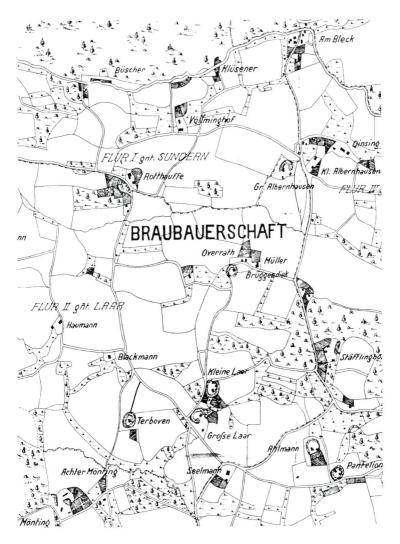

Gelsenkirchen, later 'Amt Bismarck'. Original land register of 1825
(reworked in 1925)

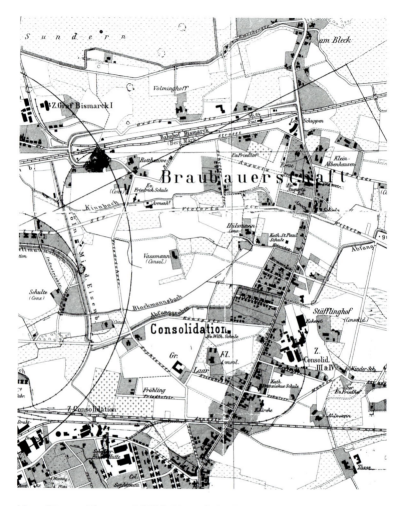

'Amt Bismarck' around 1898. Map of the District of Gelsenkirchen

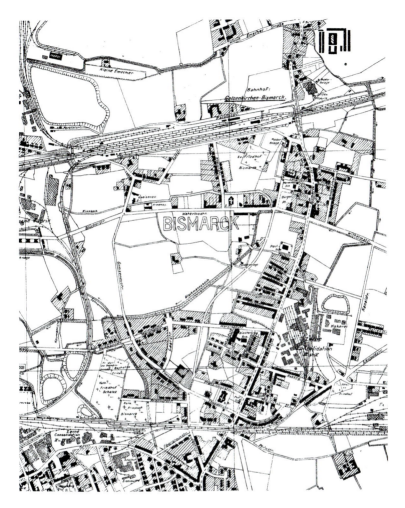

Gelsenkirchen-Bismarck in 1928

Gelsenkirchen-Bismarck, city map of 1961
Source: Land Registry Office of Gelsenkirchen

Development programme for the Bismarck/Schalke-Nord 1995

Aerial photograph of Gelsenkirchen-Bismarck and its environment,
June 1996

Source: City of Gelsenkirchen, Office for Urban and Economic Development

Chapter 3

The organisation of everyday living space

The new interpretation of the *Zwischenstadt* and the efforts to make it readable and intelligible must be proved in daily existence. In the large 'unleashed' city areas of the *Zwischenstadt*, daily life characterised by Touraine as between the extremes of 'the global-isation of the economy' and 'cultural orientation to a place', must be organised differently than in the traditional compact city. According to Touraine, the unresolved problems of the *Zwischen-stadt* reside primarily in the organisation of the spheres of activity between the orientation towards a personal place and abstract employment in the global context. They cover the social, ecological and cultural perspectives.

The conflict between 'system' and 'agora'

The *Zwischenstadt* has many faces and characteristic features. I want to reduce these to two contrasting forms: the *Zwischenstadt* as a rational 'system' of production, of socio-cultural provision and consumption on the one hand, and on the other as an 'agora', perceived as a living space for face-to-face encounters, perceptual experience of reality and direct engagement. The rational 'system' signifies globalisation and the 'agora' is the concept of a cultural, place-specific space for living, to combine two concise concepts of the Swedish geographer Gunnar Törnqvist from the Hägerstrand School with Touraine's concept of intelligibility.[65]

Both concepts – system and agora – must be understood in the light of the changes in societal structure which will have pro-found consequences for the evolution of the city. The changes are characterised by the urban sociologist Rainer Mackensen as follows:

> The trends of change include the dissolution of the old social [class] structures and their replacement by variable lifestyles, the dissolution of location-specific communication structures and the distinctions of social networks determined by roles and lifestyles, the evolution of household structures from expanded families into small, individually oriented and institutionally open households while selectively maintaining family communications and support structures.[66]

This characterisation corresponds to the dissolution of traditional social features referred to by Touraine and further accentuates the thesis of the divergence of social and spatial structure. As Mackensen argues:

> A common denominator of these findings and their lines of development is their *ambivalence* with regard to *spatial arrangements*. The evolving social structures can no longer be projected seamlessly onto patterns of spatial organisation. On the contrary, the social-spatial projections of the social differences and relationships onto the settlement profile depict an entanglement which can only be unravelled at a higher level of abstraction which cannot be grasped in geographical terms. Lifestyles characterise persons only in biographical phases, their spatial concentration says little about the continuity of the courses of life. The networks of relationships may use the same space in the same city but have almost nothing to do with each other; these circles of family and friends prove to be widely diverse.

As a consequence, the city and urban society as socio-cultural entities dissolve as Touraine had already ascertained and the living space expands to the scale of the *Zwischenstadt*. Mackensen continues:

> This must also have consequences for our understanding of forms of settlement. The 'unity of the city' is no longer based on social ties. The 'local community' is no longer 'the reduced

representation of society', no longer the place in which society can be adequately experienced. On the contrary, the empirical space extends over wide areas, but comprises them only as place-specific fragments rather than comprehensively.

The other side of the coin, he points out, is this trend's effects on the social quality of the neighbourhood:

> Conversely, the individual citizen has no longer much to do with his neighbours. The problems are mainly located at a more general level; and as each person exists in a different 'action space', his problems are mostly different from those of his/her neighbours. The location is thus neither the common denominator of social relations nor that of social experiences.

The *Zwischenstadt* is both a result and a tool of this social development. Due to the lack of centrality, the *Zwischenstadt* can be read as a system which permits the widest variety of action spaces and connections or as a 'menu' with the help of which its inhabitants can put together for themselves a life *à la carte*, provided they can afford it. By means of a rapid transport system, inhabitants can reach and connect with a large number of diversely specialised uses and places in a short time. The connecting channels of the streets and railways, the transfer nodes of railway stations, airports and goods' distribution, but also spaces which are only used for a brief period, such as hotel and conference complexes, are among the 'non-places' of which Marc Auge[67] says that they serve solely the purpose of instrumental linkage, but lack any qualities as living spaces.

In today's context, this 'mode of interpretation and this pattern of use presuppose the use of the car, as there is a lack of public transport that would provide adequate access to all areas of the city. Read and used as a 'system', the *Zwischenstadt* is thus problematic from several perspectives. It exerts stress on the environment, it does not serve those sectors of the population which do not have access to a car, and it fragments living space and living time.

The operational and technical efficiency of all supply, education and leisure facilities, of hospitals, workplaces and markets has further exacerbated our need for the car. It has led to nodal and linear concentrations of facilities and therefore to an erosion of local facilities in many urban areas in which it will soon be impossible to sustain basic provision centres accessible within walking distance. The *Zwischenstadt* is becoming more and more dependent on the car.[68]

The old planning solutions of hierarchically structured provision centres with facilities providing for day-to-day requirements located in the residential area itself, with installations for monthly needs sited a tram's distance away in the district centre, and with highly specialised, not often used, facilities in the city centre no longer work. The lower levels of supply have been dissolved and assimilated into higher ones. This applies likewise to education, medical provision and retailing. The minimum sizes of facilities have increased enormously in favour of higher efficiency, commercial viability and specialised possibilities of choice, while at the same time the density of the population in the catchment areas has been constantly falling. No end to this process is yet in sight. Both developments contribute to the increase of distances between client and supplier. In the past few years, this trend, exemplified, for instance, in shopping centres and leisure parks, but also discernible in large-scale comprehensive schools and hospitals, has shown a dramatic increase. It will perhaps be possible to adjust this development to some extent, but no more than that. Even telecommunications will not be able to achieve much here.

In this interpretation, dominated by economic theory, the *Zwischenstadt* is viewed as a major production and consumption system and thus as a part of the system of global economic integration, in which specialised and spatially dispersed divisions are coupled and connected technically in order to realise the greatest possible saving of time. Everything outside the activated connections of the relevant system becomes, in principle, invisible. The result is that those groups of the population who contribute neither with purchasing power nor with employment power or particular knowledge to the operation of this production and consumption system have only a marginal role to play in the *Zwischenstadt*. Essentially, they do not have a place in it. With increasing structural unemployment, however, these people will constitute a substantial part of the population. This also means that this view of the *Zwischenstadt* as a major production and consumption system will lead to the fading-out of all qualities which do not directly contribute to its technical and commercial function. These include the quality of experience of routes which are perceived merely as technical tools for overcoming time and place and not as part of the unity of living space and living time. In principle, this applies to the public space as a whole, as far as it is not instrumentalised for the purposes of the market.

With the systemic nature of the spatial elements, the living time of their users and operators is also more and more completely systematised, because the differentiated division of labour demands a rigorous and largely pre-scheduled control of time.[69] The constraints of a 'just-in-time' production and delivery chain are only one example of this.

The increasingly comprehensive economic instrumentalisation of time and place can only be given up by withdrawing from the globalised economy with its division of labour, and no society is able or prepared to pay this price. This means the easy way out is blocked.

Solutions must be looked for in three other directions. One is in the redefinition of the relationship between near and far. Another lies in the agreement of the limits between self-determination and external determination through the division of labour. Last but not least, solutions may be found in a new demarcation between local supply and solidarity on the one hand and the overall social responsibility of society on the other. In this complex problem area, the control of which will be so decisive for social stability,[70] the global 'system' must be challenged by the local 'marketplace' or agora. Thus, the system of the global economy must be opposed by the agora of local economic cycles, the system of abstract communication must be set against the agora of lively debate, and the system of the bureaucratic power over society as a whole must be confronted with the agora of local community and neighbourhood responsibility.

The *Zwischenstadt* will, even if this is not desired, be the locus of imported and internally produced poverty, the control of which will be the benchmark in a democratic 'civil society'. The *Zwischenstadt* as agora must also provide: space for forms of living which conflict with the globalised economy, for the slowness of an unmotorised existence and for a withdrawal into self-sufficiency in times of crisis. The quality of the *Zwischenstadt* as agora will have to be measured by its value for individual people and social groups and thus will have to provide for the specific needs and activities of the individual.

Individuals and groups of people will experience only a tiny fraction of the *Zwischenstadt* as a place of proximity, slowness and personal life. The *Zwischenstadt*, considered as a space for personal existence, is composed of innumerable individual territories which can be spontaneously connected and separated.[71] These individual living spaces must therefore have qualities of wholeness, although each of them will comprise different qualities in response to different lifestyles.

The *Zwischenstadt* will accordingly polarise into a global system of production, supply and disposal as part of the world-wide division of labour and into a world of immediate experience of perception, personal encounter with family and friends and self-determination. This polarisation applies both at the level of those who are in economic terms successfully integrated with reduced working hours, and at the level of those who are in economic terms temporarily or entirely marginalised.

For the rising number of those excluded from the global market economically, the *Zwischenstadt* as an agora is critical for survival. As has already been outlined, its quality as agora forms a basis for insuring against times of crisis, in which self-help and personal neighbourhood solidarity must be available.

The system and the agora tend towards separation and isolation. However, in the interests of a good quality of life, they must be drawn close together, indeed often superimposed on each other. In terms of the day-to-day world, a good concurrence of system and agora is critical for the survival of working mothers and fathers or those requiring care. In this context it is important to develop new imaginative models for improving tele-working opportunities, seeking cooperation between specialised hospital and domestic care, developing travel associations for getting to work or for shopping, or in creating open universities with telecommunications support and local tutorial groups. Working mothers who are bringing up children alone are exposed to the tensions between the two spheres, in some cases almost to desperation, and their case shows us particularly clearly how important a humane connection between the system and agora is.[72] The current trend, unfortunately, is still towards constantly growing separation between the two. How difficult it is to improve the situation is shown by empirical studies on trends towards individual, insular lifestyles.

Day-to-day living becoming insular

For the social, economic and commercial reasons already described, the *Zwischenstadt* confronts its inhabitants as 'man-made nature' in the form of an urbanised landscape or a landscaped city, in which everyday life takes a different course from that of the Old City. In the village, and in the traditional small town, the immediate environment provided all life resources: the garden, the shop, the school, the doctor, the priest, relatives and friends. Life operated in concentric circles: house, yard, street, district, city, region. This ideal was still pursued in the concept of the garden city and in the 'well-ordered and dispersed city'[73] – organised on the principle of neatly interlocking semantic levels of neighbourhood, district, and city – which until a few years ago represented the official planning ideal.

Historical development, and with it the reality of day-to-day living in the *Zwischenstadt*, has outgrown these ideals. This is well expressed in the following sympathetic and illustrative description by Hartmut and Helga Zeiher in their work *Places and Times for Children*, which depicts the preceding rather abstract and conceptual discussions graphically:

During the sixties and early seventies, in all residential areas spaces became increasingly specialised and specialised spaces were detached from one another. The streets were more and more characterised by increasingly dense and rapid car traffic: roads were straightened and widened for fast traffic, open spaces were turned into car parks, and pavements were narrowed. Instead of dispersed corner shops, supermarkets appeared. The inner cities were taken over by commerce and services. In the old cores of small towns, many farming and craft businesses gave up, others expanded and built new structures on the edge of the town. The small, narrow towns were particularly affected by the increasing motor traffic. The inhabitants worked less frequently than before in their town, did less shopping there and pursued hardly any leisure activities and communication there.[74]

This dissolution of social relations from the place also corresponded to a specific 'alienating' aesthetic. Hartmut and Helga Zeiher continue:

> In the spaces devoid of function new efforts to design emerged. Straightening initiatives and the reduction of nature to cultivated parks show how even aesthetic standards, determined by the range of goods on offer and the promotion of tourism, had effects on the specialisation of space. Unreflected use was replaced by distanced scrutiny and judgement. What previously had shaped in a self-evident way the visual appearance of villages and small towns, the rural and historical, now became added on to the modernised as decoration.

This development towards specialisation and separation is not restricted to towns, but also includes the countryside. They continue:

> Finally, reference should also be made to changes to entire landscapes. Here too, functions have been segregated. There are areas which have become specialised for the purposes of mechanised agriculture, characterised by division into large fields, straight, hedge-free asphalt roads and canalised streams. Other areas have been turned into leisure landscapes. 'Nature parks', 'holiday parks', 'recreation areas' were appropriately tidied up, built on and provided with rules for use. Woods were given access roads and car parks, were furnished with fitness trails and picnic areas.

This vivid description portrays the emergence of a spatial framework for life that is becoming increasingly insular. As a faithful representation of a society which is becoming specialised through the division of labour, day-to-day living is now organised in spatial and temporal 'islands' with specialised functions. These are predominantly linked with each other through traffic routes which, for the most part, do not provide any quality of life. Even the life of small children is played out in specialised locations such as the playground, the kindergarten, the day-nursery, the school, the sports club, the music school. These are usually connected with each other by streets which are dangerous for children and on which small children up to the age of ten depend on adult company for safety.

The process of life becoming insular in more and more spheres and across greater and greater distances continues in later youth and even adulthood. The spheres of activity have changed: from concentric circles into specialised points of space which are connected with the home in a star formation by inanimate traffic areas and thus 'dead' travelling times. This star-shaped configuration can also dissolve into a larger number of centres of living, which indicate a nomadic life style in the city. Commuting times up to two and three hours a day between home and work are not unusual in many metropolitan agglomerations.

This form of organisation of day-to-day living has led to the impoverishment of and a decline in the significance of the immediate environment. Also it is too strongly determined by general social factors to be changed in principle, at least in the short term. One must use all means to seek to restructure the immediate environment for small children in such a way that it can be discovered and assimilated independently as a living space in a wider, concentric expanse. However, for older children, the old unity of spatial proximity, activity and events is already irretrievably lost because that generation already makes use of a rich resource of specialised facilities, which are not available in close proximity to home. Cycle paths and readily accessible public local transport can ensure that children from the ages of 8–9 can reach these facilities independently without risk.

Studies of people's spheres of activity on ordinary working days and on Sundays, even of people with significant spatial and temporal freedom, have shown that the non-motorised spheres for shopping and walking have a maximum radius of little more than 1 km for shopping and 2–4 km for walking. If within this radius there are no attractive services and recreational facilities, it is usually the car, and not local public transport, that is used to escape. Even children depend upon this mode of transport. This means that free, unspecialised leisure time, even going for a walk, has become insular.

One should perhaps stress again the network structure of access so typical for the *Zwischenstadt* and the distribution of highly specialised functions to various centres, each placed at different locations according to their own economic 'norms' of access and catchment areas. This network structure enables inhabitants with a car to compose their personal metropolis *à la carte* in the form of highly specialised islands of activity. They exclude, however, those without access to a car – and even in our highly motorised society they account for more than half the population – from a self-determined use of the *Zwischenstadt*. This problem cannot be resolved by conventional local public transport, because the diffuse character of urban areas does not lend itself to a conventional economic railway or bus operation offering a frequent enough service.

However, the general problem cannot be reduced to whether or not one has access to a car. What is at stake is the quality of life and development for groups of the population that are disadvantaged for various reasons: e.g. children of 'incomplete' families and also the growing number of old and handicapped people who can no longer cope with a 'system-oriented' life yet at the same time do not have the traditional safety net of the family or the community. How the *Zwischenstadt*, in the sense of its agora character, can be organised in such a way that its cultural and economic diversity can be exploited by the disadvantaged in our society is an open, unanswered question. A very good benchmark for its quality as a living space, as agora, are the requirements of children and youths. This would involve: *Zwischenstadt* which is good for children and would also be good for adults and the elderly and at the same time would also have ecological advantages, because it would have to be organised around everyday living space in such a way that it would be possible to use it, to a large extent, without the conventional motor car.

Today one of the largest unresolved problems resides in the organisation of the local public transport system, most likely because our imagination is blocked by the overbearing conventions of 'bus and railway' versus 'car'.

The hopes for a reduction of motorised traffic through telecommunications are not taking us any further. It must not be assumed that communication by the media will replace all that much in the transportation of persons and goods, because

> the combination of more people and more cars, in conjunction with more leisure time and more potential destinations, will

result in a mobility structure which is scarcely or, to be honest, not at all reducible. In this respect, one also finds hardly any support for the alteration of the modal split between public and private transport. It is maintained that information technology provides the means for the replacement of journeys by electronic information exchange. No research justifies this assumption. On the contrary, many studies have shown that people who work at home, usually between 35 and 50 years old, free-lance and with a good education, choose to live in small towns or in the country with beautiful landscape and near a golf course. These people do indeed drive less often, but longer distances and always by car.[75]

Karl Ganser takes the following view on this problem:

Of course it makes sense to bundle together as much transport as possible, where the spatial conditions permit, in order to make better use of the existing public transport. And of course, everything should be done to bring about the largest possible number of workplaces, shops and schools can be reached on foot or by bicycle, even if there are relatively restricted limits for this – as we have shown.

Karl Ganser continues:

The settlement structure which is currently available in agglomerations is geared towards public transport in the sense of mass transport. To achieve this in the *Zwischenstadt* would require gigantic investments with high subsidies or a huge resettlement initiative around mass transportation stops stations. Both of these are equally utopian. So many of the hitherto pursued public transport strategies have been proven to be an irreparable subsidy drain. The transport of persons in a 'small vessel' with the greatest possible freedom of choice of time and destination will continue in future to generate the bulk of traffic. Here, the 'car' in principle has the advantage. Its ecological threat is overcome if this car acts as a means of public transport with a high level of occupation with low or renewable energy. Also it will need much less road space than is at present available in the large agglomerations. We will see a time in which there is a lot of space on the roads, without new roads being built.[76]

We seem to be further removed than ever from the implementation of such a traffic policy: effectively we are experiencing almost everywhere the unrestrained advance of the private car. This is also one of the reasons why we are at present moving still further away from the ideal of the vigorous and tangible living world of the agora. The official land use planning policy of the Federal Republic and the regional planning policies of the federal states proclaim as an undisputed goal 'decentralised concentration', 'mixture of functions' and the 'city of minimum travel distances'. However, the real trend – as we have shown again and again – is running almost precisely in the opposite direction, towards greater dispersal, more monofunctional concentrations and an increase in car traffic to the disadvantage of local public transport.

That it is the case not just in Germany is shown by the following quotation from Sweden:

> In Sweden, as in many other highly developed countries, the urbanisation process has been stable since the start of the 1970s. In geographical terms, however, we have had the same experience as North America. The general lifestyle which we have developed is connected with the pattern of distribution of all facilities over huge areas. This development is derived from the change from a production-oriented into a consumption-oriented society – from a production into a consumption landscape.[77]

On the same subject, Häussermann and Siebel state: 'Households are today completely dependent on a differentiated and widely integrated network of transport and delivery systems, which facilitates a comparatively comfortable lifestyle but enforces a way of living which damages the environment.'[78]

Day-to-day action in the 'fine grain' of the *Zwischenstadt*

There is a consensus that this development cannot go on unchecked. In future, if crises are to be survived, the planning and design of city regions must be oriented towards sustainable development and to a comprehensive cyclical economy. This is a new task, which requires different tools and procedures than planning oriented towards growth. For this purpose, a new type of planning must be developed, which is responsive to the change in dynamic.[79]

Even if the *Zwischenstadt* hardly grows much more or may actually shrink, this should in no way be equated with stagnation. The restructuring of the economy and society is continuing unabated and with it the further differentiation caused by the division of labour in the city region. It is growing together into an economically integrated space. This situation means ongoing changes at the level of everyday living. Yet with the help of traditional planning tools, these changes are difficult to plan and control both at the level of the local community and the city regions, because for the most part the changes are comparatively small-scale measures for reutilisation, reconstruction, expansion, repair and modernisation. This involves working in the fine grain of the *Zwischenstadt*.

In addition to the major tasks of the restructuring of the countryside and the major projects which continue to crop up in regions that are hardly growing at all or are in decline, the real change will have to come about through innumerable small but necessary steps of maintenance, repair and renovation. The handling of multifarious disused spaces, revaluations, interpretations and re-exploitations of disused resources all become important planning tasks, and they are to a large extent also essentially *cultural* tasks.

Public space is of particular importance for the ability to experience the *Zwischenstadt*. The creative coordination of the innumerable individual steps of day-to-day city restructuring of the public space – with the aim of achieving a perceptibly improved coherence – is both an urgent and long-term task that remains unresolved. 'Acting "in the fine grain" undermines the existing planning tools such as the regional plan/area development plan or city development plan/land use plan or landscape plan, but also the general traffic plan of the old school.'[80] What is required is a new perspective to understand and implement small-scale day-to-day tasks of planning as components of a long-term restructuring strategy. First of all the significance and scope of these old tasks, which have to be related to a new context, must be made perceptible, to enable them to be seen in a new strategic context.

The persistent, small-scale and only in the long term effective work on the reality of the inter-city requires to be corroborated by generating visual conceptions which show where small and imperceptible measures should lead. The principle of sustainability must be implanted in the consciousness by using key images, before it can be implemented in reality.

> Behind the visual conceptions, guiding images such as 'intense, imaginative perspectives' with 'substantial formative power' operate to balance between *viability* and *desirability*. They are used for *orientation, coordination* and *motivation*, and in the combination of these functions they can have a key guiding role for implementation.[81]

Images have the quality to convey and transport not only quantitative and qualitative information but also emotions and moods. They are just as suitable for making comments with multiple meanings and are thus a good resource for communication in day-to-day living, because they can constitute a bridge of understanding between different interpretations. Good images can aid orientation, they can bring people together, and they can focus on and inspire interest in a plausible goal.

The ongoing shaping of the image of the *Zwischenstadt* through day-to-day planning measures is therefore an important, indispensable task, but it is not without the danger of abuse and error.[82] Potential dangers lie in manipulation through advertising or education. Attempts to interpret the complexity of the city region through impressive images can easily lead to more or less superficial advertising images or to a type of brainwashing, which can be counterproductive. Any influence on perception must be able to be measured against the strict benchmarks and political basis outlined in Chapter 2 and the seven theses on the significance of the legibility of the *Zwischenstadt*. The reason for this is that the images serve an altered, activated perception and therefore also assist the political debate on an appropriate future for the *Zwischenstadt*.

In this process of a multi-layered day-to-day appropriation of the *Zwischenstadt* through the innumerable routines of day-to-day living and working and through workshops on local history, folk memories and tourist curiosities, people will form subjectively differentiated personal images which depend on their place of residence, sphere of activity and interests. However, these images remain linked by important shared characteristics. Mental images control and colour our perception, they can serve to amplify, to promote specific signs of our environment as symbols of dynamic change and to combine them with images of the future, which are based more on a change of meaning than on a real and already accomplished structural change. They stand for the 'principle of hope' for a changed world.

The Rhine–Main Regional Park

The plans for the Rhine–Main Regional Park support the vision to create from the open spaces between individual settlement areas, a landscape which has developed from topography and history, is oriented towards the city areas and can be perceived as a whole. This new landscape could give the predominantly anonymous urbanised area a unique form.

The eastern part of the Rhine–Main area with Rodau-Nieder-Roden. At the upper edge of the forest is Dietzenbach

Rodgau in the eastern part of the Rhine–Main area. At the lower edge of the image is the small River Rodau

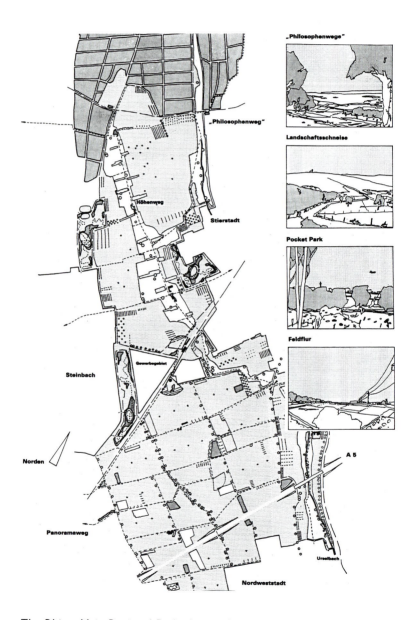

The Rhine–Main Regional Park, designed as a public 'network' in the landscape to the north-west of Frankfurt

View from the north-west over Frankfurt-Höchst. On the right of the image is the Jahrhunderthalle

Chapter 4

The *Zwischenstadt* as a focus for design

The urban periphery, the urbanised countryside or, as we call it, the *Zwischenstadt* is generally regarded as the essence of a lack of culture. The traditional benchmarks of high and popular culture, and likewise of the cultural landscape and natural beauty cannot be used to measure the possible cultural content of the *Zwischenstadt* nor to do justice to its creative development potential. Different sources and perspectives need to be examined in order to be able to grasp and develop the *Zwischenstadt* as a focus for design.

Approaches to cultural interpretation and design

To open this section, I quote from Fritz Neumeyer, because this gives a clever and competent view of a conservative approach. If one wants to qualify the *Zwischenstadt* in design terms, then it is necessary to mount good arguments against this approach:

> In matters of the modern urban landscape, the available range of tools for creating correlations, for finding approaches to designing what inherently lacks form is not exactly overwhelming. There is the great traditional approach of playing with 'figure and background', which has been significant for the city plan since the baroque era. . . . However, this method of imposing and interpreting structure while representing the figure-background seems to reach its limits when dealing with the modern semi-urban reality. One can find this already with Kevin Lynch in his celebrated work *The Image of the City* (1960) . . . . Basically, we face modern urban patterns as help-

lessly as the first man faced the starry sky, which he started to structure for himself through the projection of mythical figures, such as animal symbols.

The new city can no longer be interpreted with the resources of the existing city or architecture, but we must start again effectively from zero, with the subconscious, as though we were interpreting ink-blots in a psychological test.[83]

Up to this point, I agree with this determination of the limits of the traditional resources of architecture and town planning for the interpretation of the *Zwischenstadt*. Thereafter I think that Neumeyer draws the limits of his own discipline rather too narrowly:

Ungers' *City Archipelago*, Colin Rowe's *Collage City* – and we may also include Venturi's *Learning from Las Vegas*, because in that work architectonic gradations are examined from the lowest level of the creation of urban identity – are basically the whole range of critical tools which we have available, if we deal with the periphery of the city and at the same time with the periphery of our own discipline.

So far as concerns our urbanised countryside, we are moving intellectually in an impossible area. The prospect that presents itself to our 'eyes which do not see' is hardly more than the irritation of having either a correct concept of falsehood or a false concept of correctness.

What Fritz Neumeyer regards as an apparently insoluble contradiction, characterised by his sadness at the loss of the compact city in the open countryside and the evident ugliness of the urbanised countryside, must be taken as a challenge to search for new ways of interpretation and design in order to transform the correct concept of falsehood, as justified criticism, into the right concept of correctness, of an appropriate design.

As a critical analysis, albeit admittedly based on the traditional benchmarks of architecture and town planning, the comments of Fritz Neumeyer are useful and necessary; however, they do not get us much further than where we are today. It is precisely a constituent characteristic of this type of urbanised landscape that it has nothing more to do with the categories of architecture and town planning. Ways out of the dilemma must therefore be looked for outside the domain of the 'architecture of the city', for example, W.I. Neutelings *Reconnaissance in Wonderland: A Journey through the Periphery of the Netherlands* shows a completely different perspective.[84] The *Zwischenstadt* is perceived and interpreted quite differently, as a summary of a discussion which took place in Milan in 1989 shows and whose essential arguments are characterised by Pierre Luigi Nicolin:[85]

> Giuseppe Campos Venuti, working as a town planner in various Italian cities, sets out clearly his position, which lies completely in the tradition of reformist urbanism. For Campos, changes in the periphery, such as the elimination of decay, of dependency and other negative features which are peculiar to the periphery, such as the lack of meaningful transport systems and infrastructures, are of vital importance in maintaining the city.
>
> For Campos the sick part of Italian cities is the periphery. Comprising two-thirds of the total built fabric, it is a threat to the healthy parts of the city. Campos's call for the active use of planning resources ties in with the interpretation of the periphery which we have described as a metaphor for dependency.

This is the traditional view of classical modern town planning. It derives, however, in this case from an understanding of the unilateral dependency of the periphery on a centre which has been surpassed by reality and is therefore no longer tenable. This is not lost on Nicolin:

> Paolo Portoghesi regards the periphery as an incomplete part of the city, as an organ suffering from loss of memory, whose illness has marked the fate of the periphery. Accordingly, its reunification with the organism of the Old City should be approached in such a way that it can stimulate the capacity for remembering.
>
> The introduction of public space, for example a number of new squares, could bring the periphery closer to the core city, which is most conspicuously embodied by the Old Town, the true source of Italian cities. By means of his criticism of the

periphery, Portoghesi exercises, at the same time, criticism of the modern era. For Portoghesi, therefore, the periphery is a metaphor of the modern era. His recommended solution pre-supposes a postmodern view of history.

This view is partially correct in dealing with the lack of intelligible open space and legible history. He proposes, however, a cure which cannot work, because of its scale which is diametrically opposed to that of the historical Old Town. Nicolin continues:

> For Bernardo Secchi, town planner and theoretician, periph-ery is an inadequate term to describe something which does not fall under any definition. So he emphasises that to an increasing extent the periphery is losing the character of an area which distinguishes itself by second-degree activities and decline. Rather, it is a border area, a place in which the exchange between the city and the rest of the world is played out.

In my opinion, here is an attempt to generate an up-to-date inter-pretation, with a sense of the special role of the periphery as medi-ator between 'place' and 'world'. This unbiased interpretation forms an essential basis for further work, because it refers to the fact that, as Nicolin puts it, 'in our modern society a comprehen-sive and complex fabric of differences is being made'.

This 'comprehensive and complex fabric of differences' can hardly be comprehended through sensory perception. Despite its almost completely man-made materiality, the *Zwischenstadt* confronts its inhabitants as something alien, different and un-available. It is legible almost exclusively as a topologically comprehensible field of partially directly experienced, partly abstractly understood correlations, as a collection of areas which are only partially visible but must be present in our consciousness in order to be appropriately supplemented from it. The *Zwischenstadt* is constituted of more or less dense areas of activity, characteristics, appeals, signs, messages and recollections, of stable and elusive elements, such as an old village on the one hand and a mobile home settlement for new city nomads on the other.

The day-to-day elements of the *Zwischenstadt* lie somewhere between these extremes. These include estates of detached houses, commercial areas with a most astonishing mixture of actual workshops, but also villas, abandoned factory sheds, allotments gone wild and disused sites, discotheques and flea markets. There are also hospitals, stable yards, the remnants of old farms, woods and waterways, transmission lines, old railway tracks and dams.

A rudimentary interpretation and configuration of the *Zwischenstadt* can be found more in categories of a conception as a heterogeneous landscape, in the image of hardly comprehensible environments and ambiences, in the experience of time in its various dimensions, in the perception of atmosphere and moods, as they are conveyed in many modern films. The abrupt cuts in modern films, their fragmentation and contrasts of action, and similarly the clips of adverts without any narrative thread, serve perhaps as the most appropriate interpretative model for the *Zwischenstadt*. Analogies with the reading of texts of modern literature, or the experience of certain pieces of non-classical music, possibly lead us further on than the futile attempts to create order with architecture. For architecture and architecturally shaped urban space form only individual, important components, but can no longer determine the form of the *Zwischenstadt* as a whole.

Dealing with the day-to-day world of the *Zwischenstadt* as a cultural field of design must relate to a different aesthetic than the traditional architectural one. The cultural scientist Susanne Hauser comments on this in a different context, which relates to a critically important part of the *Zwischenstadt*, namely the process of the formation of industrial wasteland, its interpretation and regeneration. In this case, above all others, considerations of 'para-aesthetics' have a role to play, as has been developed on the basis of the works of Nietzsche, Lyotard, Foucault and Derrida by David Carrol: 'Para-aesthetics indicates something like an aesthetics turned against itself, or pushed beyond or beside itself, a faulty, irregular, disordered, improper aesthetics – one not content to remain within the area defined by the aesthetic. The first syllable *para* in this context is read to mean by the side of, alongside of, past, beyond, to one side, amiss, faulty, irregular, disordered, improper, wrong.'[86] This concept of para-aesthetics could open up a view on the chaotic richness of forms of the *Zwischenstadt* which, when measured against standardised ideals of beauty, are regarded as ugly but have long ago been discovered by contemporary art. According to Hauser:

> A para-aesthetics position would render us sensitive to transitions of many types in spatial, temporal and material aspects between 'beautiful' and 'ugly', 'useful' and 'useless', 'moral' and 'reprehensible' and thus promote the understanding that the borders and limits of the aesthetic, understood in a broad sense as socially and culturally perceptible and invested with meaning and significance, are steadily expanding.[87]

Aesthetics and non-aesthetics

In his essay 'On the actuality of aesthetic thinking',[88] Wolfgang Welsch, as an interpreter of modern French philosophy, develops concepts which carry forward the expansion of the aesthetic on the basis of Lyotard's thought:

> The subject is not the ugly, the adverse or meaningless as the opposite of the beautiful – but rather the questioning of the limits of the senses, of taste, of perception beyond the beautiful, pleasing, corresponding. The objective is an aesthetic which recognises its reverse, its non-aesthetic. . . . And in this sense, it cannot be called simply the aesthetic of modern art, but that of the modern world. It renders intelligible what the traditionalists of the beautiful will never understand: that today, paradoxically, everything turns on the perception of the imperceptible, that what we need is attention to the limits of and beyond immediate perception. Modern art and modern aesthetics through numerous, obstinate and intensive steps drive our capacity for perception quite systematically outwards beyond merely sensory perception, beyond perception in the narrower sense. That is precisely what enables us to handle the non-aesthetic of this world. That is why aesthetic thinking and aesthetic experience can achieve competence for the reality of a world which is characterised both by an aesthetic dimension and also by a non-aesthetic one.

This line of thought provides a stimulus to apply it to the aesthetic aspects of the *Zwischenstadt* in which the non-aesthetic, what is normally not consciously perceived, has an excessive weight. The following extract from the thoughts of Wolfgang Welsch, from the same essay, is also stimulating in its discussion of plurality and the combination of plural forms which is necessary for the interpretation of the *Zwischenstadt*:

> After modern art developed and took over the interpretation of plurality as such, postmodern art develops a central theme on the form of this conception and turns in an emphatic manner towards the relationship of plural designs, possibilities and approaches. This enables it to acquire a role model function for a series of problems which go beyond art. In fact, it is the problem of a society composed of highly pluralistic forms of life and it must find ways as to how these forms can be combined.

This is the subject of shaping the configuration of the *Zwischenstadt* common to important problems of the present and to basic themes of modern art. Welsch continues: 'No longer the situation of plurality, but the possible associations of plural forms with each other has become a general problem focus of the present and constitutes a fundamental subject of postmodern art.'

The thematisation of the aesthetic difference also sensitises us to social situations, their differences and connections:

> For present-day society is not a uniform group but is like a loose network of heterogeneous forms. That is its reality and at the same time it describes an ideal. We need to test out its possibilities. Aesthetic thinking provides us with the necessary tools for this purpose. . . . It makes it . . . perceptible and intelligible where predominance exists, where infringements occur and where we should intervene to defend the rights of the oppressed. Functions of tracing, noticing and perceiving gain particular importance in this connection. The political culture also requires the cultivation of such capacity for perception. This is a condition of an appropriate orientation and practice in a decisively pluralistic world.

It is only the cultivation of the capacity for perception, also for the non-aesthetic reverse side of our rational-technological world, that sensitises us to the dark reverse sides of the economic and technical processes, which 'normally' belong to the non-aesthetic world and therefore cannot be perceived with emotional involvement:

> For the pure rationalist the non-aesthetisation would perhaps be welcome, and he would continue, with the good conscience that he had not overlooked anything, to pursue a line which drives us blindly from one catastrophe to another. The aesthetically sensitised person, by contrast, recognises the reverse side of the process and maps out a different route for action that responds to the anaesthetic without becoming addicted to it. Such perception is urgently needed where the dynamics of technological knowledge and the civilisation characterised by them have lost the ability to perceive and to feel and where this disjunction has produced catastrophic effects. The only protection against systematic non-aesthetic is a targeted aesthetics.
>
> Wolfgang Welsch

These considerations can be applied directly to the *Zwischenstadt*. Only the sensitivity to its great non-aesthetic side, which truly represents the result of innumerable 'emotionless' rational decisions, can stake out the way to a different handling of the *Zwischenstadt*. In this we are encouraged by modern French philosophy, to an open, almost playful handling of elements and meanings, as the following quotation from the contribution by Wolfgang Welsch, in *Perspectives for the Design of the Future*[89] illustrates:

> Derrida shows that the materiality of what is significant in the sense of the building contributes to the constitution of sense and meanings. Consequently, it is important to dispense with the obsession for the absolute and prescribed meaning, as it lives on for example in the formula 'form follows function'. Each meaning forms itself in a system of deferrals and displacements. At present and in the future the rule will be that we must allow for the context, the deferrals and displacements of the chain of significance in order to be able to recognise and play along with the game of meanings.

In this characterisation, there is a notable whiff of relativity indicating the volatility of possible meanings which we could read from experiencing the *Zwischenstadt*. The perspective of Derrida encourages us to generate active, diverse, personal and changing interpretations depending on the connections with various functions and experiences. It encourages us to a playful handling of and interaction with the *Zwischenstadt* in its partly transitional character, to a 'gentle urbanity' in an uncertain world, to provisional solutions as well as to bold experiments.

On the character of such modernity, the sociologist Ulrich Beck made the following comments:

> However one might imagine the other modern, it will be characterised in all areas by an increased quantum, probably even by a different quality, of uncertainty: as variation, diversity, dissent, conflict, but also as threat and dangers, which fall outside the standard norms of calculation.[90]

The potential ambiguity which is evoked in the characterisation of Derrida's thinking, derived from Welsch, is used by Ulrich Beck in a positive design guideline for composition:

> Reflexive architecture of the *And* discovers, broadens the history of the place into the public dimension. It says: if I cannot change society, let me at least try to influence the way in which people pass through its architectural spaces, how they perceive the sequence, the coherence of the spaces, including the contradictions embedded within them.

Much more significantly than architecture, the creative arts, dance, theatre and music have constantly been expanding the limits of the aesthetic and have shown in a pleasurable way, for example, with pop art, how to see the beautiful in the daily and the banal. Even contemporary music, which to some extent works with day-to-day sounds, makes this clear, as shown by a comment by John Cage: 'Our intention is to affirm this life, not bring order out of chaos or to suggest improvements in creation, but simply to wake up to the very life we are living, which is excellent once one gets one's mind and one's desires out of the way and let it act of its own accord.[91]

On the basis of empirical research, the Swiss aural researcher Pascal Amphoux has drawn a distinction between the sound environment, the sound ambience and the sound landscape. Starting with empirical findings, the types of assessment of the sound world a person is capable of are:

- it is defined as a sound environment (*environment sonor*), which surrounds us, with which we maintain, 'functional' relationships of production and reception;
- it is interpreted as a sound ambience (*milieu sonore*), in which we immerse ourselves and with which we enter into 'fusional' relations on the basis of our activities;
- it is perceived as a sound landscape (*paysage sonore*), which is at the same time alienating and reassuring and with which we enter into 'perceptual' relations through our aesthetic experience.[92]

These categories seem to me to be noteworthy and suggestive because they mean that the old and greatly oversimplified distinction between 'disturbing' and 'non-disturbing' can be overcome and sound can be grasped in its multidimensional effect. Do we not find here motivations, beyond the world of sound, for a new multidimensional aesthetic? Could one not make an effort to deploy, instead of the sound environment, the concept of the *Zwischenstadt* in order to characterise our varying relationship to it depending on our personal situation?

Before undertaking any active creative organisation and intervention we must not only open our eyes but also use all our senses in order to be able to grasp the *Zwischenstadt*. Deliberate engagement, perception, recognition and interpretation with the purpose of critical and, as far as possible, unprejudiced and situation-specific appropriation of our own environment must stand at the start of every attempt to shape the *Zwischenstadt*. This in turn requires an expansion of the aesthetic world, a deferral of the limits between the non-aesthetic and the aesthetic.

This means that the aesthetic, perceptual access to sensitised experience is simpler through the perception of the traces of *life* than through the world of *forms* because the perception and interpretation of aspects of the reference to the living world render the dogmatic aesthetic benchmarks imported from outside relative.

Moreover, it supplements them with the richness of the signs of animate life. This sensitisation to the traces of life lived on the small scale can be intensified into a rich ambience for the image of the *Zwischenstadt* as a structure of signs, reflecting society with its division of labour and its socio-economic and socio-cultural differentiations, which changes the cultural and aesthetic assessment of the *Zwischenstadt*.

However, such a sensitisation involves a huge amount of work on the engrained perceptual patterns in which the *Zwischenstadt* belongs predominantly to the realm of the non-aesthetic and therefore to that part of the world which, if at all, is seen without cognisant sentiment. The condition of being anaesthetised means precisely this: at the least a lack of pain, but at the most stupefaction and unconsciousness. The transformation from the anaesthetic area into the aesthetic area of sensitive cognition accompanied by feelings, associations and 'suggestions' is a crucial precondition for any design. To quote Kevin Lynch: 'Our senses may be biologically at an advanced level of development, but in social and socio-cultural terms they are "underemployed"!'

A question which cannot be answered definitively, that is rather a design task in the *Zwischenstadt* that has to be solved anew in each individual case, is the balancing of the relationship between the aesthetic of disorder and the measure of 'classical' order and familiar 'harmony' which we need in order to find our way and to feel at ease in an anarchic arrangement of things. The relationship is precarious. The 'overturning' of the aesthetic to the non-aesthetic is precisely as delicate as the fashionable glorification of an anarchic disorder. Involvement with this subject is a task of architects and town planners.

Specialist contributions from architecture and town planning

Only relatively few practising architects and town planners have considered and theoretically reflected on the design of the *Zwischenstadt* on the large scale of the city region. I have chosen the major works of nine authors or groups of authors, which I regard as important for different reasons:

- Frank Lloyd Wright, *When Democracy Builds* (1945)
- Kevin Lynch, *The Image of the City* (1960) through to *Good City Form* (1981)
- Christopher Tunnard and Boris Pushkarev, *Man-Made America – Chaos or Control?* (1963)
- Christopher Alexander, *Notes on the Synthesis of Form* (1964) through to *A New Theory of Urban Design* (1987)
- Robert Venturi, Denise Scott-Brown and Steven Izenour, *Learning from Las Vegas* (1972)
- Colin Rowe and Fred Koetter, *Collage City* (1978).

These are my 'classics', and the following works are important for contemporary practice: Peter G. Rowe with *Making a Middle Landscape* (1991), Peter Calthorpe with *The Next American Metropolis* (1993) and finally Rem Koolhaas with his essays in *S, M, L, XL* (1995). All of these works – except for Rem Koolhaas, although he also studied in England – are works of Anglo-Saxon authors, who live and work in the USA. This is no coincidence: in the USA, the dispersed city first arose, and that is where it has developed to its extremes and has been perceived as a planning and theoretical challenge, whereas in Western Europe the problem has been relatively suppressed.

In what follows, I will be attempting briefly to characterise the works in order to promote them as an enjoyable reading resource. I regard the most important of the selected authors for the forming of the *Zwischenstadt* to be Kevin Lynch, to whom, consequently, I grant most space, whereas I only give a brief characterisation of the other works.

In *When Democracy Builds* (1945)[93] Frank Lloyd Wright developed the concept of 'Broadacre City' on the basis of a fundamental critique of city and society. For him, true democracy could only be implemented through enabling personal self-determination on one's own land. The car and the modern road network had freed the city from its old narrowness and made it possible to develop it as a land-spanning and field-like entity with individual concentrations of development around the intersections of the roads.

Frank Lloyd Wright developed and illustrated his vision with large models and drawings, combined with ideas for a new education system based on practical experience, a new city area with agriculture supplying fresh produce and a new working culture. Here he was standing in the living tradition of the American dream, of the utopia of a free society determining itself and rooted in the land. This vision of a broad city landscape was in a specific respect – as we now know – extraordinarily far-sighted. The urbanised landscape has become a reality, but not in the social and economic form which Frank Lloyd Wright proposed, and also his belief in the blessings of the motor car has today rather changed to the fear of its evils. Nevertheless, his dream of Broadacre City remains one of the great classical town planning utopias with far-reaching influence.

Kevin Lynch originally wanted to study with Frank Lloyd Wright, but the pathos of the genius did not suit him. He too stands in a living American tradition. His works remain an indispensable foundation for any theoretical and practical discussion of the form and shaping of the *Zwischenstadt*. Perhaps he is still the most important theoretician for our subject.

In a period in which the social sciences dominated and the socio-cultural significance of space was radically called into question, Kevin Lynch used new questions and methods to examine and demonstrate the significance of space for the well-being of the inhabitants on the large, metropolitan and countryside scale. He extended the spectrum of consideration far beyond the examination of visual perception in particular to the significance of the experience of time and change, the significance of different environs and the particular significance of space for children and young people. His works *The Image of the City* (1960), *Site Planning* (1962/1971), *What Time is This Place?* (1972), *Managing the Sense of a Region* (1976) and his last book, summarising his views in a final synthesis, *A Theory of Good City Form* (1981) still form a rich source of observations and far-reaching thoughts for the creative handling of the *Zwischenstadt*.[94]

What was radically new about *The Image of the City*? It consisted of the essentially simple, but previously never raised question about the 'internal image', which the inhabitants have of their city: how is the city perceived, what remains in the memory, how does orientation work and what procedures of interactions between environment and occupants influence the inner attitude and perception?

According to this study, the city is conceived as the common product of the 'hardware' of the real, physical environment and the 'software' of perception and use. In the process of comprehending the city, both the 'hard' and the 'soft' world cannot be separated – the interactions between both worlds is what allows 'city' to exist in the first place. *With this insight, the city can be altered both through work on the 'hardware' of the built fabric and on the 'software' of the consciousness of the city – but the most effective way is to address the interaction itself, by directly involving the inhabitants in the reorganisation.*

Right from the start of his pursuit of the form of the city Kevin Lynch bursts the frame of traditional *urban design*, which as 'architecture of the city' is restricted to the palpable, in terms of experience principally integrated areas of streets and squares or larger functional complexes.

The form and design of the city as a whole and of its region as a living space are the binding, perception-guiding interests that pervade all his works. This interest leads him to expand the traditional working methods of the architect and to develop new methods and modes of presentation. Through this he has made important discoveries which still apply today, and that is why his work is rightly deemed to be a classic. However, in the climate of retrospective postmodernism there was no space for a humanistic planning philosophy, and in a climate hostile to planning and social reform, in which the interdisciplinary work between planners, psychologists and social scientists had largely ceased, there was no space for a social science-inspired discussion of his views and statements. Consequently neither theoreticians nor practitioners of planning and urban design have engaged with the approaches of Kevin Lynch in any depth.

The engagement with the city perimeter and city region – and therefore with the *Zwischenstadt* – on the basis of the concepts developed by Kevin Lynch expands our repertoire of design resources and our notion of city aesthetics, including the perception of the city as seen from the car, without neglecting social and humanistic conceptions of value. Kevin Lynch's discovery that the city is only to be understood as a field of interaction between the environment and the inhabitants forces us to involve the inhabitants as an indispensable corrective of any one-sided professional perspective and evaluation, and this not only in the sense of a sociological review of the analysis but more significantly in the spirit of active sensitisation and the promotion of active willingness to collaborate.

The extent of the areas to be structured and the necessary abstraction of design instructions at the level of the city and the city region require the development of new resources for plan representations. Within broad limits, such plans must be capable of being interpreted and orchestrated as codes not of design but of the design programme. In the design programme defining notation systems, which are developed before the actual design and also relate to the 'software' of the organisation, Kevin Lynch performed genuine pioneering work in *The Image of the City* and *View from the Road*.

In his last work, *A Theory of Good City Form*, Kevin Lynch brought the qualities of a good city plan down to five concepts:

1   Vitality – to be classed as life-retaining and life-promoting, but also as lively.
2   Sense – this roughly corresponds to the concept of intelligibility, legibility and ability to experience.
3   Fit – to be translated as compatibility and the balanced relationship between environment and activities.
4   Access – this corresponds to the concept of accessibility.
5   Control – this comprises the availability and appropriation of the environment and also its ability to change, preferably through the user.

All these *dimensions of performance* must in addition correspond to the criteria of *efficiency* and *justice*. They must, therefore, be implemented by the appropriate means, and must meet the requirements of social justice. Kevin Lynch did not describe his ideas as being for an 'ideal' city, but rather he repeatedly attempted to describe the city as a 'being' which can take on many forms depending on its location and culture. He put forward his vision of the city as a field of human interaction that owes many of its characteristics to the model of the 'organic city', in contrast to the oppositional models of the 'city as the depiction of heaven' and 'city as a machine'. His ideas describe his humane vision of the city as a great and endlessly diverse and constantly changing social and cultural field, which only remains alive and humane if its occupants are in a position – and also actively prepared – to play an active part in it and to engage with it.

With *Man-Made America – Chaos or Control?*,[95] Christopher Tunnard and Boris Pushkarev provided, as early as 1963, a precise analysis of the 'intermediate world' of the urbanised countryside of America. They analyse it under the motto 'An aesthetics for man-made America'. Their analysis covers the themes of the low-density residential areas, the design of motorways, the major industrial landmarks, the recreation areas and the protection of historic buildings and monuments. They combine their analysis with principles of design which, wherever possible, are attributed to the foundations of perception and these are demonstrated with many practical examples. The book remains a goldmine for the design treatment of the urbanised countryside.

Christopher Alexander with his contributions *A Note on the Synthesis of Form*, *A Timeless Way of Building*, *Pattern Language*, *The Oregon Experiment* and *A New Theory of Urban Design* (1987) has attempted to formulate a quasi-natural order for the settlement model.[96] He began with the attempt to open up the treasury of experience of human settlement history through the analytical breakdown of the human environment into under-lying structural elements or 'patterns', which are combined into complex, uniformly perceived cumulative elements and derive from the general experience of a 'common sense' for composition. This attempt is carried over to the planning and design process by means of the systematic, positive responses to each situation encountered, with the involvement of the user as the land owner.

In his philosophy of life and in his practical work, Christopher Alexander starts with a position based on mathematics and computer analysis and develops it into an attitude founded on the holistic-romantic and the Far Eastern traditions, in which beauty, conceived as world harmony or a 'quality without name', the devotion of the inhabitants and the manual construction process are intended to form a unity. This determination of the day-to-day patterns, promoting life in the dialogue between inhabitants and planners and the significance of the production process itself have a specific importance for the *Zwischenstadt*. They leave space for self-determined construction and self-determined public spaces. Even if the current attitude of Christopher Alexander reminds us of rather problematic industry-hostile romanticism similar to the

Arts and Crafts movement of the nineteenth century and although his discussion of the social and political problems of the time is somewhat aloof, he still holds an extraordinarily important position. With his system of *patterns* as basic components of the wholeness of activity and space, which at the same time acts as a linguistic resource of understanding between planners and users, Alexander has made a contribution to spatial and social arrangement which seems to be particularly well suited to the *Zwischenstadt*.

In *Learning from Las Vegas* (1972)[97] Robert Venturi, Denise Scott-Brown and Steven Izenour detail their discovery of the beauty of the vulgar commercial strips. In this regard they occupy an intellectual stance which is opposed to that of Alexander. On the basis of Pop Art, they have opened their eyes to the world of signs of the ordinary suburbs and their unique aesthetic charm. They combine a massive critique of the lack of image, symbolism and significance of modern architecture with a positive analysis of the North American commercial highway architecture, dominated by advertising signs and ornaments, and expand this analysis further to formulate a positive assessment of the 'prairies' of ordinary single family houses. In doing this they have torn open the horizon of architecture and the aesthetic of orthodox modernism substantively and effectively. They discover a new folklore, which reveals itself in vulgar advertising signs and the small-scale kitsch of front gardens and house doors. They have expanded the vocabulary of urban design, even if, in their passion for the world of advertising and beautiful appearance, they have avoided a critical look at the poverty behind it.

Coming from yet another, quite different, direction, Colin Rowe and Fred Koetter offer their perspective on the city in their influential book *Collage City* (1978). This lays new foundations for an interpretation of the modern city on the basis of the historical analysis of the roots of modernism. For a new treatment of the *Zwischenstadt*, the work contains numerous new thoughts. According to Bernard Hoesli:

> Colin Rowe and Fred Koetter start with an analysis which historically is connected to the early Utopians and is rich in ideas on the utopian content of modern architecture with its grandiose gestures and mistakes. However, they contrast utopia with traditions of another type (particularly Town-

scape and Beaux Arts) and so set out the tension between utopia and tradition.

This is beneficial for the analysis and design of the *Zwischenstadt* as well, since both together – utopia and tradition – are necessary to make the city as a whole. '*Collage City* is a call to enlightened rationality, which includes perceptual experiences and emotions, hope and memory.'[98]

Collage City has become a generally accepted concept, which tellingly circumscribes the apparent formlessness of the *Zwischenstadt* with its fragments. Unfortunately it also threatens to become yet another empty motto.

This provides a brief characterisation of my 'classics'. The following three works are more useful for immediate practice.

In *Making a Middle Landscape* (1991)[99] Peter G. Rowe provides a sober and realistic analysis of the background, historical motives, valuations and forms of the dispersed urbanisation of the USA. The thesis is that these forms of urbanisation are the consequences of an intersection of 'romantic yearning for landscape' (pastoralism) and a 'technical temperament'. Ways of designing are seen as 'poetic operations' – such as the *juxtaposition* of contrasting forms; *scaling* from unusual to ordinary objects; *ordering* in the production of intelligible orders; and not least in *typological inventions*, in the development of new hybrid superimpositions of elements of infrastructure and architecture. The historical analysis is better than the design examples, which are too shallow.

Peter Calthorpe attempts in *The Next American Metropolis* (1993)[100] to compose a manual for town planning for the *Zwischenstadt*. Again, this is strongly oriented towards the tradition of the small American town, with thoroughly integrated road networks, somewhat higher density and above all the establishment of cores in the form of *pedestrian pockets* for mixed use, which preserve the public space for pedestrians and which are linked to each other by a local public transport network. This all more or less complies with our principle of 'decentralised concentration' and is an attempt to structure the sprawl with *transit-oriented development*.

The refreshing contributions of Rem Koolhaas in *S, M, L, XL* (1995)[101] offer a sharp insight into the reality of contemporary implementation conditions in construction and planning. I cannot always agree with his rather too impassioned dramatisation of these conditions in the 'ennoblement of the existing' (Mönninger) despite one's joy in his observation and formulation skills. However, this enabled him to clarify and purify his view of reality and at the same time to provide a new outline of the limits of planning. Planning for the unforeseen and planning for intermediate spaces, not of the buildings, as the principal task. This range of themes of 'planning and room for manoeuvre' was indeed much discussed in the early 1970s, but Rem Koolhaas has resurrected it in an original manner and at a different level.

The available literature is limited, but rich in content. There are certain theoretical foundations for the design of the *Zwischenstadt*. There is also an appreciable history of ideas not only of the concepts, but also of the practical approach to the *Zwischenstadt* and its interpretation. The engagement with the history of ideas of planning and design shows how differently the *Zwischenstadt* can be interpreted and assessed and how much it depends on the mental images, which guide our perspective.

Work on the mental images

In the section 'Day-to-day action in the fine grain', the importance of images has already been highlighted. Images allow us to recognise the *Zwischenstadt* as a structured whole amidst the constant transformation that results from primarily day-to-day changes in the city. Leading images do not arise automatically, they must be shaped. They will be different for every person depending on experience, training, inclination and interests:

> Leading images are, to a large extent, mental and pictorial images. They can address various areas of life and are characterised by substantial formative power that they derive from a precise balancing of the two underlying dimensions of *feasibility* and *desirability* which in principal are subject to an inherent contradiction. Their three essential functions for society and the individual are *orientation*, *coordination* and *motivation*; in particular the close integration of these functions forms the basis for the guiding images' inherent capacity to provide us with guidelines for action.[102]

Depending on our inner attitude, the *Zwischenstadt* is also a mirror of our self-perception and a screen for the projection of wishes and critique. The work on the sensitisation of inhabitants to the *Zwischenstadt* and with it the work of positively influencing the mental images is a task which is as diverse as it is charming and unending. Urban and regional planning is called upon to participate in this work as much as those establishing culture and even sport. As a result of new trends of movement and the location of sporting events in specific areas, sports can in particular engage people who cannot otherwise be reached.

In order to approach this task constructively, it is necessary to visualise the process of perception and the way it is recorded in our memory. In this way potential graphic aids could be deployed which can form a 'memory framework' in the mind. The question should then be asked what use the computer could be in opening up the city region. One major task would be to clarify how public information campaigns ought to be structured, to ensure they are neither advertising in the conventional sense nor an oppressive educational programme.

Perception and memory

The classic perception study for the complex city configuration remains Kevin Lynch's *The Image of the City*, first published in 1960. Since this pioneering work there have been a large number of psychological studies on mental maps,[103] they have, however, hardly contributed any practically usable results and have not gone beyond Kevin Lynch's classic study.

Lynch's categories – paths, edges, districts, nodes and landmarks – remain highly workable both for perception and planning; they have proved their worth. However, now that we want to go beyond the concept of mental maps, we must bring in findings from the fields of perceptual psychology during the past few decades.

According to these more recent findings, the image of a mental map is a simplistic comparison, because perception is the result of superimpositions and the interference of at least two, but usually more, information circuits. Therefore, the more sensory 'input channels' that are used, the more intensive and sustained is the image because perception uses different parts of the brain simultaneously. Instead of comparing it with a 'mental map', comparing it with an 'internal hologram' is probably more accurate not least because people can frequently recognise the whole already in a detail, in the same way as in a hologram the whole is apparent in each part.[104]

Through intensive and repeated perception of the same circumstances 'traces' are formed in the brain, whereby the interest-guided and emotionally intensified attention serves as a filter for which perceptual stimuli will be processed.

Perceiving can proceed with different degrees of intensity – from simple instantaneous seeing, through the perception of objects, to attentive perception, up to comparative and metaphorical interpretation. In fact it may possibly extend even up to identification, in which deeper personality traits and levels are also involved. In this sense, perception can also be conceived as a process that can be built up from the superficial impression of the short-term memory through to image concepts which will build on each other to any depth of long-term memory. For the legibility of the city region, this could mean building up perceptual concepts of different types and intensities which mutually supplement one another.

Perception is all the more intensive and sustained the more senses that are involved. Accordingly, the legibility of the *Zwischenstadt* is evidently intensified if, in addition to the sense of sight and also for example of history, tactile experiences and typical sounds or even smells come into play and, as it were, designate and encode a space in several ways.[105]

To give an example, my mental image of Hyde Park in London is composed of the following elements: childhood memories of reading *Peter Pan*; images of English lawns, combined with the smell of cut grass; the sound of cars from the distance together with the feeling and the sound of crunching gravel; people reading and trying to concentrate under large trees and young men playing football; heavy, high railings and towers and large tree silhouettes. All in all, many densely integrated strands of different sensory perceptions form a complex memory, coloured by the light of an optimistic mood in which I experienced London and Hyde Park as a young man on my way to study in Liverpool.

Despite the completely different cultural connection, one could also mention the 'song lines' of the aborigines in Australia, the routes leading across a continent occupied by myths and legends. Closer to us, there are literary city guides such as 'With the eyes of Franz Biberkopf through Scheunenviertel, Prenzlauer Berg and Alexanderplatz', which are offered by young art historians in Berlin and in which literary and visual impressions are inseparably combined.[106]

Perception leads to memorability, if what is perceived is combined into a 'form', which in an ideal case should possess such characteristics as conciseness, simplicity, stability, regularity, symmetry, continuity and uniformity. For the most part, the *Zwischenstadt* lacks exactly these characteristics, and this makes orientation so difficult. All the more important are the few strong lines and points of orientation which exist in almost every *Zwischenstadt*, or which can at least be strengthened and developed.

On the other hand, the *Zwischenstadt* requires a certain illegible configuration in order to arouse curiosity and therefore interest and attention. A simultaneously balanced but nevertheless tense relationship between order and a lack of overview as a result of the labyrinthine configuration makes the city interesting in the first place.[107]

The legibility and memorability of the city region could be compared with the legibility and memorability of a musical score: 'The best way of getting a work into your memory is analysis, the recording of the formal context, sound images and the recollection of the appearance of the notes'.[108] This comment on the memorability of a musical work also fits in with the city.

The *Zwischenstadt* can also be read as an open text which demands the active collaboration of the reader with the text in order to understand and enjoy it. The urban areas in the *Zwischenstadt* are like a collusion of different fragments of text which are not always easy to understand, whose authors are generally only known by exception, with gaps which readers have to bridge with their own imagination and fill in with their own stories. However, they can, depending on their 'mode of reading', combine fragments into different sequences and interpret them quite differently depending on their mood and experience.

Memorability, even of objects of a relatively abstract nature, is obviously generally supported by the presentation of spatial elements as anchors and as stores of events, images and signs. It is here that the link with the subject of the legibility of the city is quite obvious.[109]

Graphic aids – computer support and information campaigns

The most effective mental maps are probably the factually shaped structures of drawn maps. Accordingly, the orientation diagrams simplified and intensified to logos, which display the features of 'good form', have great significance as reading and orientation aids. A classical example of this is the London Underground map, which has many worthy successors in other cities. For subjects other than local public transport such diagrams have still not been developed.

These orientation diagrams, however, must have adequately perceivable and sufficiently frequently occurring 'recognition signs' corresponding to reality, so that they can achieve their purpose. These recognition signs can in turn have the quality of graphic signs, e.g. in the form of posters, sign-posts and instructions or, better still, they should be signs in the form of real entities like church towers, industrial buildings and other monuments.

In the future, the intelligent use of the computer with clever graphics programmes and information systems will have an important role in the orientation and opening up of the cultural richness of the city region. This will be all the more so if the nature of the perception of the younger generation is more and more strongly shaped by dealing with computers and screen graphics. In the future it might be advisable to connect with these modes of perception if we want to reach the younger generation with a message which will expand their horizon of perception.

Information campaigns – for example, in the form of a systematically organised poster culture in the railway stations or as serialised columns in the local newspapers, through to regular local radio and television broadcasts – could make an essential contribution to getting to know the *Zwischenstadt*. Here we have a broad and fruitful, if still largely unexamined, field for metropolitan cultural work.

In the context of the International Building Exhibition Emscher Park, such information campaigns were prepared, for example, in the form of a 'Route through the industrial culture'. Also a series of simplified maps with pointed and captivating messages were intended to make the Ruhr area more readable and intelligible. In each case these campaigns sought to communicate an important 'eye-catching' message. Examples include: 'Orientation is simple', 'The axis of the Ruhr is as important as the axis of the Rhine', 'The new Emscher Valley: after "Blue sky over the Ruhr" comes "Blue water in the middle of the district"', 'Work and environment: we are building the new Emscher Park – it is creating jobs until well into the next millennium', 'The Emscher Landscape Park – the new tranquillity and the new wilderness in the district', 'The myths of coal and steel: on the route to industrial culture', 'Artificial mountains and technical towers: The landmarks in the district', 'Network innovation – the chain of technology centres and colleges'.

The essential messages were summarised in a 'map image' which would communicate the diversity of small urban fragments, quarters and settlements so typical of the Ruhr, interspersed with open spaces, the special form of the urban-ness of the Ruhr district.

Urban design, culture and sports policy: the example of the International Building Exhibition Emscher Park

Images alone can achieve little. The essential contribution to the 'legibility' of a city region necessitates the process of small design interventions and the creation of a meaningful environment, since legibility in the first place means – as we have been attempting to explain – consciously perceiving, memorising, recollecting. This process can take very different forms:

- Externally imperceptible elements can be made visible and accessible and therefore capable of being experienced.
- Previously not consciously perceived elements can be rendered effective and made easily remembered through 'cultural loading', meaning that they can migrate from the non-aesthetic to the aesthetic area.
- Previously emotionally negative elements can be given a new interpretation by linking them with positive events.
- Elements that have been made visible, that are positively

charged and that have been reinterpreted can be linked up to form a chain of perspectives and experience. In other words, plural, completely different signs can be combined into a region-wide super-sign.

• Information campaigns can disseminate these exemplary processes and therefore provide stimuli to the discovery of the region.

The potential for such a rendering legible is different in each *Zwischenstadt* because of their different topography, history, landscape and economy and must in each case be discovered separately. In the Ruhr area, the International Building Exhibition Emscher Park has put such processes into action, a few examples of which follow.

The so-called 'Jahrhunderthalle' of 1900 on the former Krupp site in Bochum was supposed to be pulled down because it no longer had any use. Step by step this intention was culturally whittled down until the Jahrhunderthalle became recognised as a monument and an important place for meetings and events and its future was thus secured. Werner Durth and his art students from Mainz initiated this process; they worked artistically on the site, exhibited their results in the hall and later published them in a very beautiful form. They achieved provisional public access and for the first time drew an interested public to the building.[110]

The initiative was intensified through major symphonic concerts by the Bochum Philharmonic Orchestra under their experiment-loving conductor Kloke and through major ballet performances. Both events required the securing and consolidation of public access to the building. Since then the hall has been firmly associated with the experience of cultural and sporting events; indeed, it has been restored using the funds which were originally allocated for its demolition and has now become the central point of an artificially shaped city park of a new type.[111]

A comparable process of cultural occupation was initiated for the Duisburg-Meiderich blast furnace and steelworks which were originally scheduled for demolition. Major cultural events (music, theatre, multimedia) and sports activities (diving, climbing) have been combined with events connected with industrial history and plant ecology. These all shared the purpose of creating a major People's Park through careful reutilisation and redesign of disused industrial facilities.[112]

The enormous gasometer in Oberhausen, about 120 m high and 65 m in diameter, was also originally intended to be demolished as it was popularly regarded as an ungainly monster. By making the unique interior space accessible for cultural events and in particular for the exhibition 'Fire and Flame' on the history of the Ruhr district, the structure changed from being a symbol of industrial decline to being an unmistakable landmark of cultural renewal.[113] In June 1996, it became the stage for the major international cultural event 'I, Phoenix'.[114]

An example from landscape design: in the partly technically deformed, partly geologically 'natural' landscape of the Ruhr district, agricultural technologies are used, for example, to create large coloured, geometrically arranged fields of flowers, in order to generate with the plough large graphics signs on the harvested fields and to construct unique artistic signs with the large pressed straw balls. The technically deformed deposit fields and the geologically original, natural elements are accentuated by subtle landscaping and geometrical patterns.[115]

With resources and measures of this kind it is possible to create new artificial landscapes which then become characteristic elements of the region and help modify the traditional ways of perception through initially uncustomary 'alienation', and help detect and celebrate the hitherto concealed, because they are unconventional, beauties of the old industrial landscape which is usually regarded as ugly. The citizens involved in the discussions with the artists are able to experience directly the transformation of their own personal modes of perception.

Festivals can also be used as a means for promoting regional consciousness. In 1992, the Bochum Philharmonic Orchestra, under the baton of its conductor Kloke, held a music festival of a special kind under the title 'Setting out for America', to coincide with the 500th anniversary of the discovery of America.[116] Particular places from the now ending epoch of the coal, iron and steel industries (steelworks, collieries, blast furnaces), once inaccessible 'forbidden cities' and today without function, were used for musical events. The performances were connected to a journey in which also old colliery rails and canal ships were used. This led to a major musical staging of a past world. Formerly this world could not be experienced by the inhabitants of the region; today, in a new context of experience, it has to become an essential component of the culture of the Ruhr region, if it is not to lose its historical identity.

In all these cases, the collaboration of ecologically oriented open space planning – or of city development, culture and sports policy – has led to a positive reinterpretation of old industrial facilities, visible from afar, and of destroyed landscapes. Thus a major contribution has been made towards retaining the history, orientation and legibility of the regional context.

Other examples can be cited. One slag heap was artistically moulded while still being used for deposits,[117] another was topped by a steel pyramid to make a viewing platform.[118] This way the slag heaps are perceived as points of orientation and viewing points, which open the region up to a bird's-eye view and make it legible through the visual chain of other heaps which have been shaped into signs.

Particularly designed landscape elements are connected with cultural and informational events – such as, for example, the re-development and redesign of the site of the former 'North Star Colliery' in Gelsenkirchen within the framework of a Federal Garden Exhibition[119] and the development of the 'Forest Garden Ripshorst' into a modern arboretum, which is accessed via a bridge over the Rhine-Herne canal which itself is designed as a landmark.[120] The new landscape elements form major new connection and orientation signs in the region.

The examples from the International Building Exhibition Emscher Park show how effectively the interaction of ecologically oriented open space planning and socially oriented urban development with culture and sport can be used to open up a 'forgotten' region for its inhabitants. The political fusion of urban development, culture and sport in a single ministry, as is the case in North Rhine Westphalia, can offer good political and administrative approaches and starting points for this, which have to be extended to the regional and local authority level. The entire city region must be understood and conceived as a broadly construed area of metropolitan culture, as a never-ending process of internal change and qualification.

The International Building Exhibition Emscher Park has laid the foundation for a new form of regional planning, which is no longer oriented towards growth, but to a recycling economy and inner qualification in the form of unceasing internal transformation. Surprisingly, this cannot take place without an intensive cultural permeation. If one combines the ideas of a recycling economy with the original Latin concept of *cultura* in the sense of land cultivation as well as in the sense of care, respect and occupation, then the step to considering the city region as a cultural landscape of a particular kind – of a cultural landscape in which everything, without exception, is cultivated and developed by man – is no longer a major one. To stay with the notion of agrarian land cultivation which over many centuries was a high art of maintaining an ecological balance: such a cultural landscape ought to be cultivated as a whole as a densely populated landscape networked in a multiplicity of symbiotic cycles. This landscape must also include fallow land as an important intermediate state between nature and culture. In the FRG, a major condition for this is the currently discussed further development of the 'Land Use Ordinance' into a general 'Use Ordinance', which also comprise areas without buildings.[121]

Planning in a city region that is consistently aimed at sustainability and a recycling economy would incorporate the process of dealing with land use cycles and therefore also the various forms of fallow land and their intermediate uses and restorations to new use. This procedure has – next to and frequently even before functional and economic aspects – a cultural, an artistic and an ecological side. The briefly outlined examples from the Emscher region show that frequently an ecological and artistic occupation and 're-coding' of fallow land can take place prior to the economic and material restoration.

Stimuli for this procedure of re-coding can be found in modern art in multiple forms, for example: the interpretative emphasis and rendering visible of elements of daily life through altering the context or the scale; the opening-up of the concept of artistic work to include open, unresolved processes; the combination of different types of art into 'installations', etc. These are examples of artistic processes which have changed our view of the world and which continuously promote the mutation of the anaesthetic into the aesthetic.

This altered view must also influence our approach to the *Zwischenstadt*. Landscape planning, town planning and urban design must once again form a conceptual and creative unity. They must, as planning culture, enter into a discussion with art and general cultural theory.[122] In this sense, they must themselves again become an 'art' and be understood as major components of a metropolitan culture which conquers the *Zwischenstadt* as its field of operation.

The example of the International Building Exhibition Emscher Park for a cultural occupation of the *Zwischenstadt*

The illustrations show examples of the cultural occupation of former industrial installations which hitherto frequently gave rise to negative feelings. Their new cultural interpretation makes them positive signs of structural change: at the same time they incorporate the special history of the region and point with their new uses towards the future.

The Landscape Park Duisburg-North, the former Thyssen Meiderich smelting works. Concert in the open foundry hall

Source: Photo International Building Exhibition Emscher Park/Peter Liedtke

Gasometer in Oberhausen: with a diameter of about 65 m and a height of approximately 120 m, it is today probably the largest accessible internal space in Germany. Below and above the mighty lid, formerly 'floating' on the gas, the space that is illuminated only by the small roof lights is used for exhibitions, musical performances, light and laser shows and experiments

Source: Photo by Manfred Vollmer

A lift takes the visitor up to the roof platforms, which on three sides offer a broad view over the former industrial landscape which is in the process of conversion

Source: Photo Thomas Brenner

The Zollverein XII colliery, built in 1928–1932 by Schupp and Kremmer, which in its entirety has been listed as an historical monumental, is to be used as an art and culture centre after the structural fabric has been secured

Source: Photo Thomas Brenner

The enormous hall of the former Krupp steelworks in Bochum (the Jahrhunderthalle) has been converted into an auditorium for artistic meetings, congresses and regional festivals

Source: Photo Stefan Ziese, March 1993

Land Art with 'bat tents' in Mechtenberg

Source: Photo Thomas Brenner

The slag heap in Bottrop has became the 'Emscherblick' viewing place, crowned by an equilateral steel pyramid: a new landmark after the gradual disappearance of the hauling towers and factory chimneys (Architect: Wolfgang Christ)

Source: Photo Thomas Brenner

'Change for People' – the conference of the International Building Exhibition Emscher Park in the Jahrhunderthalle in Bochum, May 1994

Source: Photo Thomas Brenner

Chapter 5

Perspectives for a new form of regional planning

At the start of the final chapter, the comment by Karl Ganser on the Emscher region from the 'Memorandum II' should once again be quoted, but this time in its complete form, because his comments are generally applicable to and relevant for the *Zwischenstadt*:

> The settlement belt of 800 sq km in the centre of the Ruhr district is a built-up area. With the weak growth potential of future times this *Zwischenstadt* – which neither complies with our image of the city nor with our yearning for an intact landscape – can no longer be remodelled. We must accept it as a given and endorse its hidden qualities. We must create order and draft images which will make this encoded landscape legible. This could lead to the development of a new type of regional plan.[123]

We will try to outline such a new type of regional plan. For the new task of dealing with the *Zwischenstadt* we need a new planning culture. Our intermediate conclusion of the fourth chapter was that city and landscape planning should conceptually combine and should again become 'arts'. The artistic–architectural tradition of *urban design* in town planning must be united with the tradition of garden and landscape architecture of the baroque era and the great landscape parks of the nineteenth century, and both traditions must be combined with the traditions of forestry and agriculture which have always been oriented towards 'sustainability' and long-term thinking and acting.[124] *The open space of the landscape will become the actual creative field, which must preserve and restore the identity, the unique character of the* Zwischen-stadt. Developing the built fabric in its fixed typology can make only a limited contribution to this.

These different traditions of urban design and landscape architecture, however, require a creative impetus through mutual fertilisation, because at present they persist in segregated pigeon-holes and a conceptual freeze. They are, on the one hand, narrowly formalistic, on the other, determined by natural science and ecology; they are either fixated on the pre-industrial city and landscape images or lack any aesthetic sensitivity. There are too few creative superimpositions between aesthetics and science – much has to be done for the entire field to become once again intellectually lively and creative.

What conclusions derive from this for practical regional planning? The methods and tools of regional planning for a region with relatively low or without any growth must be different from a planning methodology which in the past had essentially to distribute increasing growth. Regional planning which today has to control primarily qualitative changes, reutilisations and reinterpretations – and that in fields of action the range of which exceed by far that of individual communities – must restrict the old traditional set of tools on the one hand, but expand it on the other to address fields which have been far remote from regional planning hitherto. Regional planning must change from being a predominantly restrictive, controlling and distributive activity into an active and creative one, which requires its own political and financial basis in order to be able to make the region qualify as an integrated field of action.[125]

Conceptual models for the development of the intermediate city

Before we turn to the action areas and tools that regional planning will need in order to deal effectively with 'fully-grown and fully developed *Zwischenstädte*', it is useful to outline what development models are conceivable. Regarding the structure of settlements, Hanns Adrian, the former Municipal Town Planner of Frankfurt and Hanover and President of the Deutsche Akademie für Städtebau und Landesplanung (German Academy of Town and Country Planning), has defined four categorically different models which conceptually delimit the field of possible developments.[126]

Model 1: The preserved city

All resources and tools will be used to retain the basic structure of the city. The inner city is structurally and architecturally most attractive. It is predominantly a pedestrian area, but it can also easily be reached by car via bypasses and general car parks. Public transport covers the entire surface and is built to a high quality. With major planning efforts and very extensive intervention the development of a dispersed settlement form and centres remote from the city is prevented.

(Hanns Adrian)

Such a prevention of dispersed city growth could only be implemented by draconian interventions which could hardly be achieved in our democratic, freedom-oriented society and would represent encroachments on the self-determination of the communities and of people, on the land property market, the traffic and transport economy and the free choice of residence which could not be democratically legitimised through constitutional law. At present, only undemocratic societies can still enforce a compact city.

Model 2: The city of co-operating centres

The inner city remains the most important shopping area, although supplemented by specialist markets integrated into the development structure and by shopping centres to supply the regionally dispersed settlement areas. The city centre remains multifunctional. It becomes a predominantly pedestrian area and is accessed by radial routes of public transport. It remains accessible for vehicular transport which is, however, reduced to the essential. The inner city is deliberately developed for its competitiveness: expansions of variously qualified and expensive locations, targeted city marketing, intensification of department stores, introduction of integrated malls and close interconnection of the inner city with densely inhabited areas.

(Hanns Adrian)

This is the model which is at present pursued by most cities in Germany, strongly influenced by the pressure on local authority policy of the jeopardised inner-city retailers. As already briefly indicated, however, this frequently leads – hardly noticed by the public – to an erosion of the historical substance and thus to the loss of the very character of the inner city which makes it so irreplaceable in cultural terms and for the creation of the identity of the city. The gradual destruction of the historical centre takes place, leading to the degeneration of the historical buildings into advertising and mood-creating façades for the retail industry.

Model 3: The emaciated city

In the areas surrounding the city very large high-capacity shopping centres emerge which take over the supply of the region and the city for the most part. Through the preservation of monuments and historical buildings the inner-city can be largely maintained and retains its attraction for tourists. City and region become permanently car dependent.

(Hanns Adrian)

This is the development which we can observe in particular in the 'new' federal states of the former East Germany, where the large shopping centres at the edge of the system-built housing schemes of the 1960s and along the motorways continue the draining of the historical inner cities which was already systematically being pursued by other means in the time of the German Democratic Republic. On this, Hanns Adrian comments elsewhere:

Above all in the East, the lack of a civic awareness of the city and a local civic capital base is one of the causes of the expansion of the 'developers and investors'. The cities are becoming just financial investments. More and more, the once very important regulation of social integration of building owners and businessmen is missing.

Here, a return to the policy under Model 2 seems, in many cases, no longer possible, but for all its problems, the release of the historical inner cities might perhaps offer the opportunity to maintain their historicity and to develop them into high-quality special residential areas. It is, however, rather questionable whether and how the new peripheral shopping centres in the eastern part of Germany can, in terms of urban design and landscape, be sensibly integrated at all into a *Zwischenstadt* – and this would arguably be a precondition for the development of the historical inner cities into special residential territories.

Model 4: The city of artificial worlds

> The region is supplied by a system of specialised and optimally functioned centres which can be reached and are connected through a perfect, region-wide traffic network: shopping centres, office centres and open landscape are developed into quality entertainment centres. The old city cores also acquire the function of this kind of 'centre'. They are destined to form adjusted and managed artificial worlds. The historical city continues to exist only as place-specific stage settings.
>
> (Hanns Adrian)

This evolution is taking place in a relatively pure form in the USA, but there are also first signs of this kind of development in Central Europe. Shopping centres are being enriched with cinemas and offer entertainment venues; they host the stagings of popular cultural events and link up with artificial experience-worlds of the likes of Disneyland, with substantial entertainment parks, with 'fun pools under palm trees' and with refined technical game-worlds for children and young people. It is not yet discernible whether this currently booming development, which consumes very large plots of land and generates a huge amount of car traffic, is to be replaced and surpassed by some other fashion. As Hanns Adrian puts it: 'The poorer the real world becomes, the greater are the opportunities for monofunctional artificial worlds.'

I am convinced that the policy and range of tools of spatial planning in our form of society are too weak to prevent this type of artificial world. If isolated campaigns against it have been successful – as, for example, in preventing the artificial world of a German 'Edmonton Mall' in Oberhausen – then, immediately after the exhaustion of the publicly concentrated defence, the 'New Centre of Oberhausen' is pushed forward as a somewhat smaller but nonetheless still very large shopping centre. At present, not much else seems to be possible than stubbornly pursuing the objective of a close connection and penetration of day-to-day living with culture and landscape, with experiences which are integrated in day-to-day living. We must be confident that the tide of 'artificial worlds' will eventually ebb. A glance at the USA shows that there are counter-movements there (e.g. the New Urbanism), which could very much be compared with our principle of 'decentralised concentration'. There the planning targets seek to bring about pedestrian pockets with higher density and mixed use as cores of a 'transit-oriented development', connected by light railway systems or accessed only by special roads for buses or for cars with at least three occupants.[127]

Conceptual models and planning concepts are necessary, but what will be decisive for a more human development of the *Zwischenstadt*, will be the relationship of people to their fellow human beings, to the cultural quality of their city and to the nature of their environment. Without 'ploughing' the field of the *Zwischenstadt* in respect of its social, cultural and ecological quality, all technical and economic efforts – of this I am convinced – will at the end of the day remain fruitless. An indispensable condition for any such 'ploughing' is a new political and administrative conception and constitution of the *Zwischenstadt*.

The necessity of administrative reforms at the regional level

The reality is far removed from a political and administrative reform of the *Zwischenstadt*. Regional planning in Germany is stagnant, in intellectual, scientific and administrative terms and above all politically. In order to avoid the semblance of an academic argument which is all too remote from reality, I will continue to stay with the seasoned practitioner Hanns Adrian.[128]

> Administrative reforms at the regional level are long overdue. The present regional planning authorities were set up in the sixties and seventies. Their abilities to control regional development are based on the principle of consensus.
> By now, the conflicts between core cities and peripheries

have become so severe that for many topics agreement on the basis of consensus is no longer achievable.

The conflicts have to do with the funding of regionally significant facilities, the retention and maintenance of open landscapes, the social segregation between the Old City and the periphery and the migration of businesses from the core cities into the hinterland, usually with negative consequences for the core cities. Local authorities in the 'bacon belt' around the core city are thriving, but for other areas of the *Zwischenstadt* the conflict can expand to catastrophic proportions.

> The periphery can only be protected against further destruction if reformed regional planning authorities can implement plans despite objections of individual cities or communities.
>
> If we consider with what courage the Prussian reformers almost 200 years ago granted the local authorities the right to self-administration and the right to exercise power, it is shameful how the subject of 'regional self-administration' is being avoided. We need a reform of regional administration and its planning authorities and councils which grants them power of coordination and gives them the right to manage conflicts with legitimated power.
>
> (Hanns Adrian)

Today, regional administration would certainly have to have a different character than, for example, the old Prussian sovereign administration of the nineteenth century – it would have to be more oriented towards procedures of moderation and towards the balancing of interests and contracts with the private sector than to the implementation of sovereign and central decisions. Nevertheless, regional councils would have to be given important decision-making power and this would include their own budgets and their own immediate and direct democratic legitimation.

The realisation of an effective regional self-administration with decision-making power and budget control will encounter resistance in particular from the wealthy communities in the *Zwischenstadt* which profit from socio-economic segregation, and for that reason the individual steps to regional self-administration must be carefully considered. As Hanns Adrian suggests:

A first step could consist in transferring to the existing regional councils on a larger scale, and at a larger rate, tasks of implementation in addition to their planning tasks. The Kommunalverband Großraum Hannover [KGH, the Greater Hannover Council], for example, is responsible for public transport in the region as a whole and for establishing and operating local recreation facilities. The regional councils could bit by bit take over responsibility for regionally significant facilities. The KGH, for example, has been running Hanover Zoo for a year and could very easily become responsible for many other facilities, for instance for theatre and opera.

This start would, however, soon have to be followed by broad political legitimation, in the form of the introduction of a regional parliament with direct elections. The Region of Stuttgart has dared to take the step towards establishing a regional parliament, and the development there should be carefully watched and assessed.

In the end, under the aegis of the association of regional planning authorities, a growing number of partnerships of convenience could be set up, possibly with different area allocations, to deal with a large number of tasks. This could allow for the theory that the areas of responsibility can no longer be unambiguously determined, but that depending on the task there are 'oscillating fields' (Siebel).

(Hanns Adrian)

With the introduction of a regional parliament, an important step will be taken to setting up true regional cities, with a two-level local authority administration: the region will elect a council directly and with it a 'regional mayor'. The distribution of power between individual local authorities and the region must be agreed in accordance with the local and historical situation, but in any case the regional city must have the right of budget. It will be the bearer of all the facilities of importance for the region and will exercise planning sovereignty (which it can to some extent delegate), and it will take over implementation tasks and must take over the tasks of the sphere of influence assigned to it, including tasks which previously belonged to the district councils.

> Within the region there are [either local authorities with altered competencies] or city districts with directly elected city district councils and district mayors to which the greatest possible amount of responsibility will be delegated. This organisational structure has precedents in the city states of Berlin and Hamburg.
>
> (Hanns Adrian)

The establishment of regional cities is an urgent requirement, in order to prevent the consolidation of wrong developments or, where possible, even to reverse them:

> The development and colonisation of the regional peripheries is progressing more rapidly than the development of the core cities, which succeed far too slowly in mobilising their building land reserves. Many people are dispersed to the periphery of the region because cities no longer permit suburban residential environments and development patterns at their edges. The periphery is in danger of losing its qualities and of suffocating in a cemented ring of uncontrolled industrial settlements, haulage contractors and shopping centres.
>
> (Hanns Adrian)

Regional cities must develop over the years their own regional consciousness and understand that the strict separation into the core city and periphery can no longer apply: 'The "core cities" must enter into competition with the "peripheral city" by making their own attractive offers for the development of their hinterland, and the "periphery" must also offer "city" facilities' (Hanns Adrian). Above all, however, both are responsible for the preservation and timely transformation of the open land:

> For the major cities, the interfaces between city and countryside are of inestimable value. *In the next few decades, the protection and development of green areas and the open land surrounding the city will gain the greatest significance, comparable with the task of saving the urban quarters of the cities*

from destruction through restoration. The quality of the cities is measured not least in terms of their embedding and integration in their landscape.

(Hanns Adrian)

This is a new task that can only be managed through the integration of agricultural and forestry policy into the planning of the city region. Although the right of environmental protection already gives far-reaching initiatives, it is too conservative in orientation for a task which demands the transformation of the landscape and not merely a protection of open spaces. To turn to Hanns Adrian again: 'To an increasing extent there are regional plans which take on this task, but it is not enough to protect open spaces. The task consists in consciously designing, shaping and forming the landscape [as a component of the *Zwischenstadt*].'

A more precise analysis of existing potentials – which would only have to be combined with regard to plan and objective – would in many landscapes close to the city reveal major opportunities for landscape design. Adrian gives an example of this from Berlin:

In the north-east of Berlin, for example in the area of the former sewage fields (an area for major city expansion), a 'landscape conference' discovered that in such locations, which are so typical of major cities, an astonishingly large number of authorities, departments, city estates and associations are active and also have resources for investment and maintenance. Their coordination alone could produce enormous potential for change.

In these new forms of landscape integrated into the *Zwischenstadt*, there has to be also scheduled space for forms of housing and industry which cannot be integrated into the classical city:

The particular attraction of suburban residential environments resides for a large part in the broad leeway for the individual to implement his residential dreams. This applies to Black Forest, Friesian, Bavarian houses as much as to arbours which have been developed into castles and to all houses which have been built through self-help, with materials pilfered from construction sites, and with grandma's savings. Suburbia is an area of retreat for threatened active and exotic urbanists. This function can hardly be achieved in integrated urban areas. In contrast, it seems to be generally problematic to transfer typically urban settlement forms – for instance those derived from city structures of the period of promoterism – to the *Zwischenstadt* for which new typological forms have to be developed in response to living forms and industrial patterns existing there.

(Hanns Adrian)

A problem which remains unresolved is that of traffic, in particular access to all areas of the *Zwischenstadt* by public transport:

In the periphery, one can drive by car to our heart's content. Often one even has to. This produces car-dependent suburbia and the city proper, accessed by public transport, side by side and less and less connected with each other. Park and ride places which could provide a connection are opposed on more or less valid grounds.

(Hanns Adrian)

Conventional buses and railways are suitable for access of areas in the *Zwischenstadt* only in few areas, and there is therefore a need for intermediate forms between private and public transport to be developed: 'Already today this is unlikely to be achievable without close integration of individual and public transport. Equally important is the linking of peripheral settlements with each other, for example through close-meshed and comfortable networks of bicycle paths' (Hanns Adrian).

Up to now the *Zwischenstadt* has been ignored as a unique form of urban development and as a major planning and design task: as a nameless entity it is not a 'concept'; in political terms it breaks down into many individual local authorities and communities and is consequently not conceived as an integrated field of policy. For regional planning, with its imperturbable belief in the order-generating effectiveness of its 'central place theory' or its theory of 'decentralised concentration', the beautiful categorical imperative of Christian Morgenstern applies that what shall not be cannot be.[129] Adrian comments on this:

No doubt, we must also take conscious note of the dramatic development of the periphery of our city regions. The old tools of regional planning are no longer able to procure ordered and sustainable conditions. New strategies are required. Their most important elements are:

- A regional administrative reform which makes the development controllable again.
- Accepting suburban forms of living as part of large cities. We must give them space.
- Large-scale and sustained protection and development of important landscape.
- The core cities should not rely only on the impact of restrictive regional planning tools. They must aggressively expose themselves and open up to competition.' (Hanns Adrian)

The city region of Stuttgart

The space of Stuttgart shows the development of a *Zwischenstadt* particularly clearly. The various settlement areas – five administrative districts with 179 municipalities – have merged with the multifarious landscape into a regional city whose individual locations can be reached from each other by car or train in a maximum of half an hour.

The regional city shows a distinct network structure and a decentralised cultural diversity in association with the attractively structured landscape. This has enabled the space of Stuttgart to evolve into a multiple-centred metropolitan region, with eleven regional city components each of 150,000 to 200,000 inhabitants, each with their centres and with different 'features, aptitudes and qualities' which are mutually complementary.

These regional city parts could constitute the basis for an administration, close to the inhabitants and at the same time performing well, as the administrative level of a regional city with its own constitution.

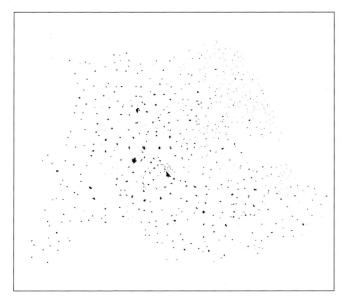

Stuttgart and its surroundings in 1850

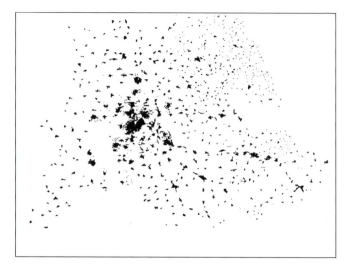

Stuttgart and the Central Neckar Area in 1950

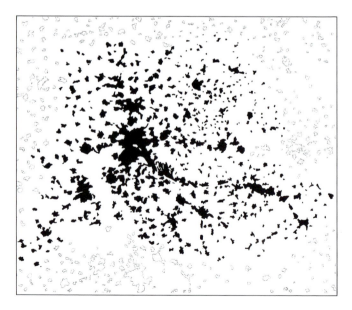

The region of Stuttgart in 1995

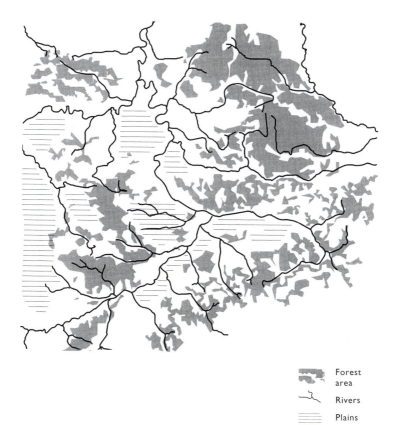

Forest area

Rivers

Plains

The region of Stuttgart: topographical diversity

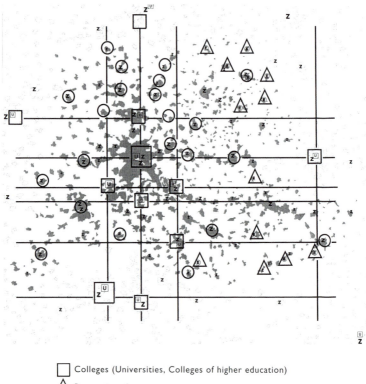

◻ Colleges (Universities, Colleges of higher education)
△ Recreation place
○ Culture/history

The region of Stuttgart: cultural diversity

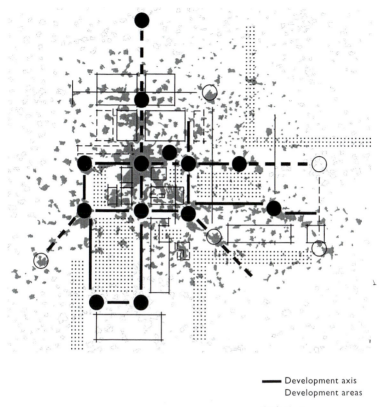

▬▬	Development axis
	Development areas
⊞	Settlement
⣿	Landscape
○	Development focus

The region of Stuttgart: network structure

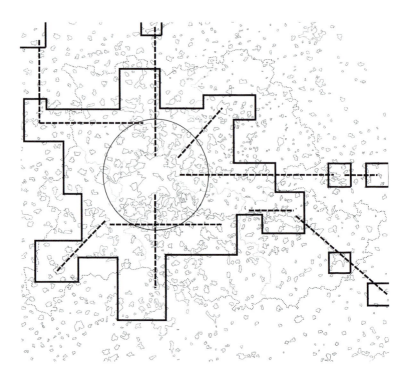

The region of Stuttgart: organisational structure

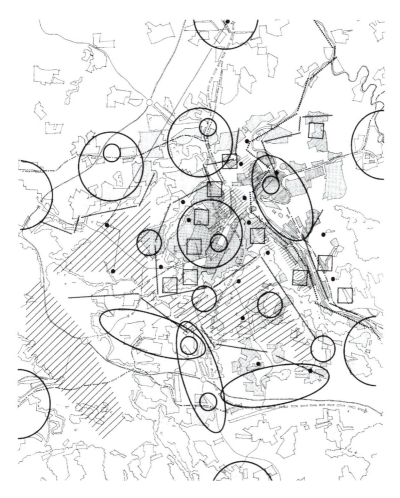

The region of Stuttgart: regional districts/regional district centres

Fields of action and tools

There are many ways, measures and projects for qualifying the *Zwischenstadt* with the existing financial resources and even without growth, to transform it and to include it in a comprehensive recycling economy. I regard the qualification of the intermediate city as a particularly gratifying political task because, with political imagination, procedural creativity and the promotion of an innovative environment, there is much that can be achieved.

One could summarise the tasks of a new kind of regional planning of the scale of the *Zwischenstadt* into five major fields of action:

1   Transport and Communication
2   Protection, Care and Development
3   Transformation and Expansion
4   Orientation and Information
5   Culture and Sport.

The first area of action, 'Transport and Communication', forms the instrumental basis for the transformation, functioning and development of the *Zwischenstadt*. The objective of this field of action should consist of the integration of different forms of transport and communication into a single system in which targeted actions can take place with medium-size vehicles that operate at higher capacity. Such a system would also include the space-traversing technical media on the one hand and networks for 'slow traffic' operated by muscle power and possibly with support of solar energy on the other, because both together must combine with motorised traffic in order to minimise the latter and promote a settled way of life.

The second field of action, 'Protection, Care and Development', comprises essentially the classical areas of the protection of landscapes and historical monuments. It involves the preservation of the natural and cultural heritage and the experience of the temporal continuity in geological, biological, historical terms (and in terms of a life experience over one to two generations). Consequently the protection and maintenance of landscapes and historical monuments and cautious further development must stand in a balanced relationship to each other, so that the historical experience of the depths of time is not 'suspended' and lost but can be perceived in its dynamism and remains open to the future.

In addition to the 'classical' fields of action of the protection of landscapes and historical monuments, further fields can be embraced by the notion of protection and maintenance, for instance that of environment and ambience, also in terms of the preservation and careful maintenance of areas under reduced pressure to cultural and economic adjustment, areas in which time moves in a way more slowly, as in slow motion. In the action area of protection, care and development a retarding and decelerating element is included to some measure. It operates on the principle of the smallest possible intervention, deliberates on the scales of different biological periods and metabolisms as well as on periods of history, and it can determine ecological and cultural areas in which no planning should intervene, but which are left to themselves and should regulate themselves. (The paradox of the plan: planning for what cannot be planned for.)

There is an important area of overlap between 'Protection, Care and Development' and the third field of action, 'Transformation and Expansion'. This relates to areas which are on the one hand to be protected from active development planning but can on the other develop under certain circumstances a strong development dynamic precisely because, for them, specific regulations are suspended and in all the intensity of regulating development is reduced. Unplanned and unintended, but intensely vital and 'urbane' areas of this anarchic kind can be particularly observed where, for example, legally imposed road intersections (or other planning law decisions) have not been carried out but have remained in force, in some cases over decades, and have caused an obstacle to investment for the relevant construction project. Under the umbrella of the endorsed but never realised plan, informal but tolerated activities of many types can develop which otherwise would not find an economic niche. As Rem Koolhaas has found, a specific form of urbanity prospers apparently only through its illegality. In such areas the new can be tested out, developments can be initiated and alternative lifestyles can be tried out in a quasi-anarchic manner. Consequently, such areas belong to the field of action 'Protection, Care and Development' as well as to that of 'Transformation and Expansion'.

The actual field of 'Transformation and Expansion' is, however, the area of the simple and complex projects with the help of which new developments are encouraged and which also structure the diffuse city as focusing stabilisers and spatial anchors in the form of centres or edges. This field is characterised by an urging, rapidly altering momentum, but can also be characterised by an ambience of 'time acceleration', as a 'percolator' for the transfer of new knowledge, abilities and products into the region, for example, in the form of new technology centres and associated commercial areas.

Across the preceding fields of action spans that of 'Orientation and Information' which is responsible for the long-term coherence of the *Zwischenstadt*, for the network of paths, signs, lighting and signposts. Across the various areas it is responsible for attractive paths, good orientation and complementary information, also for good information through a very wide range of media outlets.

'Orientation and Information' overlap in turn with the fifth field of action, 'Culture and Sport'. The task of this field is to bring about, through cultural initiatives and sporting events, the reinterpretation of specific areas that are perceived to be emotionally negative or neutral. This area is also responsible for the celebration of 'times and places' with regular regional festivals and highpoints, distributed over the year and, in some circumstances, changing location, in which it is possible to experience the *Zwischenstadt* as an overarching totality.

The tools of such an altered regional planning can be divided into three major groups, which can be classified from 'hard' to 'soft' tools. The tools do not coincide with the fields of action, but on the contrary they overlap and also represent connections between the fields of action.

1 *Planning and operating regionally significant infrastructures*, such as public transport, supply and disposal; regional cultural facilities, such as the zoo, the theatre and opera house, as well as major open-air auditoria. A specifically important task is the development and maintenance of new regional parks as landscapes which are structured deliberately on the broad scale, with ecological agriculture, with new 'wildernesses', and with the development and maintenance of long-distance hiking trails and cycle tracks.

2 *Securing, controlling, designing and developing regionally significant public spaces, buildings and areas.* This includes the securing, planning and design of regionally significant open areas and public spaces, the targeted coordination of ongoing repair, conversion and reutilisation measures for regionally significant elements, the identification and promotion of regionally significant renovation and utilisation areas and, not least, the initiation and promotion of projects of particular regional significance, in the spirit of 'bridge building, node strengthening and network intensification', as Peter Zlonicky has so pertinently described it.

3 *Information, communication and participation.* These tasks include the drafting of clearly memorable orientation diagrams, the development of simple computer programmes which can be used to 'open up' the region, the awareness of people of unusual, concealed qualities through the various resources of public visual information (poster campaigns, etc.). This would also include contributing to local newspapers, local radio broadcasts, regular television broadcasts with regional information, and – possibly in the context of a regional academy – the offer and organisation of excursions, seminars and workshops and the organisation of design workshops and regionally significant cultural events.

All three types of tools endorse major, regionally significant measures. Cultural initiatives aimed at stimulating symbolic reinterpretations (of, for example, negatively perceived industrial brownfield sites) and the reinforcement of meaning in the form of exhibitions, cultural or sporting events will be followed by formative planning and could also (but do not have to) lead towards the adoption of operational responsibility by the new regional administration.

In contrast to the traditional planning approach, the new regional planning is distinguished mainly by its very much stronger cultural approach and commitment and also the adoption of apparently small but, in total area and time, significant regionally effective repair and conversion measures. It is possible, for example, that through skilful modification and appropriate connections the installation of a forest path can in some circumstances also become part of a long-distance hiking trail; or the repair or relaying of a cable or pipe can offer reasonably priced opportunities for the redesign of a regionally significant street since it has in any case to be resurfaced; or the closing down of an industrial firm can suddenly offer up new possibilities of design and development.

With the vision of a new cultural urban landscape and with an altered administrative and political structure, regional planning could open up a perspective on a new planning culture with creative tasks and could therefore become a highly attractive design field, capable of attracting the best political and specialist talents.

Regional planning of this kind, particularly if it takes over operational responsibility, can – this cannot be emphasised enough – only be fully effective, however, if it has its own political power and budget basis. This is indeed the only way in which the necessary regional self-awareness can grow.

Open questions

In the Foreword, I referred to the dilemma to which the train of thought inevitably leads, if the questions raised here are not taken up and answered step-by-step by citizens, politicians, culture and science and by the planners. In such a case, only the criticism of traditional concepts, the myth of the old images and the weakness of urban and regional planning will be perceived, *and not the major formative perspectives which open up with the criticism.*

At present, it seems that political optimism is not appropriate – urban and regional planning and urban design rank right at the bottom of the political agenda of important questions. Ecological problems are suppressed under short-term economic objectives. Any cultural discussion is still under the influence of the old historical patterns. The practice and science of urban and regional planning are both equally unproductive. The long-term commercial prospects indicate a rather more modest role for Europe, with all in all strongly reduced resources for urban and regional planning and urban design.

However, I nevertheless incline to the hope expressed in the Foreword that for its ecological and social crises society will find well planned answers to questions which have been asked in time and placed in a perspective context. It is, however, probable that the need for this will first have to become much greater, before the necessity for such action is realised. For this reason, the following questions must be taken up with the necessary scepticism. I order them on the basis of three conceptual areas which form the sub-title of this book: the *Zwischenstadt* between place and world, space and time, town and country. They summarise the area of discussion.

The Zwischenstadt *between place and world*

The globalisation of the economy is severely restricting the possi-bilities of action of the nation–states and also of cities and communities. Their financial leeway is largely dependent on con-stellations in the world economy and the financial conduct of the multinational companies. A restoration of the old European inter-vention state cannot be expected, at least in the perceivable future. In place of this, city contracts, public–private partnerships and balance of interest through moderation procedures will gain greater importance.

The local authorities must therefore look for new routes and areas of self administration in order to maintain their social peace and cultural identity while at the same time struggling for inter-national competitiveness.

But how can the local environment, the small local and regional economic cycles, and the social and cultural ties to place and local communities be strengthened as a complement to internationalisa-tion? Can one expect that in the long term, under the rise of globalisation, the local cycles will also be strengthened? How can cities make an effective contribution at all to preventing the social uprooting of economically marginalised groups? What types of public space, what communication structures, what local net-works must be built in order to hold together the groups of popu-lation which are drifting apart from each other in economic and social terms? How, for example, can it be ensured in practical terms that privately financed and publicly subsidised housing can continue to be mixed together? How can the particular local iden-tity be protected against the tendencies towards international sameness and indifference without falling into small-mindedness? To put it briefly, how can cities pass the test between achieving international competitiveness on international level and retaining social and cultural individuality on local and regional level?

The Zwischenstadt *between space and time*

> At present, the bad thing is that only time or speed or the lapse of time exist, but no longer any space. It is now necessary to create spaces and occupy them against this acceleration.
>
> (Heiner Müller, 1995)[130]

There are indeed signs of acceleration and the loss of space affecting all circumstances of our day-to-day living: individual isolated living and working islands are being functionally linked by the fastest possible means of transport, which use ugly tracks through inhospitable 'no man's land' and for their part are linked with transitory, fleeting 'non-places'. It is no longer the spatial distances, but the expenditure of time in transit and the costs of information transfer which determine functional structures. For instance, the new 'Transrapid' train, had it been realised, would have linked specific parts of Hamburg and Schwerin temporally closer with the West End of Berlin than many districts of Berlin itself are today. Completely new space–time maps are being created, which have hardly anything more to do with old topography and history. Admittedly these maps apply predominantly to people involved in the structure of global economy; the other larger part of the population is still living predominantly tied to a location. Furthermore, for the new space–time network there is a high ecological price to pay in the form of energy consumption and the cutting up of the landscape.

The question is whether there is any significant political and economic interest at all to promote, through increasing the 'resistance to space' (in particular for the car), the local environment as a city of short paths and thus of pedestrians and cyclists and to enhance at the same time local and regional commercial activities. Is it not the case that the economic policy of the European Union, together with its traffic policy, is going exclusively in the opposite direction? To put it briefly, how can the space of real sensory perception and lively social contacts, the public space as stage, workshop and home, be protected against the dominance of the rapid overcoming of spatial distances, measured in abstract time and information?

The Zwischenstadt *between town and country*

The city is integrated with the landscape, and the old contrast between town and country has already substantially dissolved in favour of a city–landscape continuum. This is a fact which can hardly be changed by criticising 'urban sprawl' and promoting the planning principle of the 'decentralised concentration': 'Key words such as land consumption, settlement sprawl, bacon belts, etc. also indicate the consequences of inadequate perceptual models which, in connection with exclusively functionalistic planning concepts . . . have not produced a positive formative power.'[131]

Where, however, are there promising approaches for placing the highly subsidised agricultural policy at the service of the forming and shaping of the *Zwischenstadt*? Are corporations and regional authorities at all able to grasp the task of a comprehensive shaping of city–country integration as a social and cultural continuum and exercise the power to make this task a political topic? Who, from the Federation and the *Länder*, will pay for this? What are the prospects of civic movements in this area?

Finally, an optimistic dream: could it not be possible that, under pressure from ecological problems, the vision of a new cultural city landscape – as a resource in inter-regional competition and as a long-term and sensible measure for creating employment – would become a topic as popular and as widely politically supported as, a generation ago, the protection and regeneration of the historical city cores?

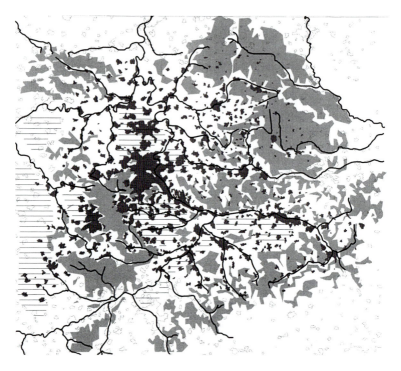

The region of Stuttgart. Fine-grain interpermeation of forest areas and settlement areas. The picture shows also the water courses and — hatched horizontally — the plains

Postscript to the second edition

The city in the Second Modern Age

The fifth chapter and the first edition of this book ended with some open questions. Some of my students have taken this as an occasion, in the context of preparing for their examinations, to draft a description of their position regarding their future role in the professional field of town planning. Frequently, the works of Ulrich Beck and Anthony Giddens have been used as a reference, a sign of the fact that students can once again look beyond the horizon of their own discipline. In fact, the temporal diagnoses of these two sociologists working with the concept of a Second Modern Age make a contribution to giving a productive interpretation of the *Zwischenstadt* as a field for planning action.

The key concepts developed in their various writings[132] in the last few years – essentially ecological and civilisation risks as a consequence of modernisation, globalisation, individualisation and alteration of the employment world and post-traditional society – can be applied productively to the situation of town planning.

Ulrich Beck sees in the – undesired – side-effects of modernisation the essential factors for the structure and progress of the Second Modern Age. In fact, the current practice of town planning could hardly be more accurately described than as dominated by the side-effects of modernisation. Only a few striking examples need be given of this from the areas of traffic planning, landscape protection and economic promotion.

In the construction of new traffic installations, for instance, for noise protection, relieving the city core and parking spaces, the issue is almost exclusively the removal of the deleterious side-effects of the traffic structures originally built to promote the development of the economy and of society; these installations to combat side-effects in turn cause a chain of further side-effects.

The intervention and compensation regulation devised to maintain the natural basis of life does not pursue any independent formative objectives of its own, but is only used for the laborious calculation of the ecological balance of the side-effects of development projects; when systematically applied, such an approach leads to an unhealthy separation of ecologically dead construction areas and ecologically patched up landscape areas, with their corresponding new – unintended – side-effects.[133]

The efforts to protect traditional retailing in the historical inner cities against the side-effects of the competition of retail parks outside the gates of the city lead to a temporally delayed but obviously unstoppable adaptation of the inner cities to the structure of the shopping centres and therefore to the destructive side-effects of the draining and destruction of the historical city cores. The few examples mentioned illustrate this: town planning and spatial planning have become defensive, they are attempting to defend the old structures with unsuitable means and are yearning for old images, without realising that the traditions themselves have become so empty that they are incessantly breaking up. Anthony Giddens clearly shows[134] that we have reached in the Second Modern Age a period in which society and city have to live without the support of historical conditions. This can also be vividly demonstrated by the example of the city: the recourse of postmodernism to building history and what is known as 'critical reconstruction' of the old cities become stale already after a few years; the old traditions and rituals of a halfway homogeneous cultural urban society are dissolving into culturally unassociated and incompatible individual elements, which can no longer be brought together through an overarching 'master plan' in the spirit of traditional urban development.

Beck and Giddens clearly show how the unstoppable economic globalisation in interplay with the worldwide media is contributing to the dissolution of local, place-specific cultures and thus to the devaluation of place and space as emotionally and symbolically charged foundation of an urban society which considers itself to belong together. Furthermore, with globalisation the power of community, city and regional authorities to control urban development effectively is being undermined from outside as well as from inside. In addition to the defenceless exposure to a global economy, there is the dissolution of the old solidarity of urban communities as a result of the disintegration of classes, strata and traditional families. What is left are inhabitants who are more or less isolated and are forced into an individualistic way of life which often has to be newly decided upon short-term,[135] and public authorities whose problems can no longer be resolved within the boundary of their communities.

The individualisation of forms of life as a result of the dissolution of collective ties has winners and losers, and this is apparent in particular in the alteration of the world of employment. The dissolution of the Fordian working world and the lifestyles standardised by it, the massive loss of simple industrial jobs with long-term secure employment, is driving all those less qualified, who cannot cope with the new information technology, into – often permanent – unemployment, or into short-term and badly paid occasional jobs.

Urban society is exclusively held together by the shared risk of dependency on a highly complex and vulnerable technology: noise, air pollution and traffic sprawl affect poor and rich alike, even if not to the same extent.[136]

The old European town which constituted a contrast of town and nature is dissolving, with a trend to technically conditioned equalisation and the expansion of unhistorical 'non-places' around the world.[137] This development seems – not only under the diagnosis of time of the Second Modern Age – to be irreversible, although nobody can predict its specific future formation in social and spatial terms.

In view of its structural problems and uncertainties, how can town planning find a way from its present resigned position restricted to the defence of exhausted city tradition? This is neither possible by sticking with the old control tools of state intervention, developed in the Golden Age of the national industrial state – for lack of the golden rein and due to the changed problem structure these tools are leading less and less to their goal – nor by preaching further deregulation, which sees the salvation in unrestricted exposure of the city to the free play of an intelligent but enlightened market. All considerations on appropriate prices, reflecting the ecological or cultural shortages of natural and cultural assets, remain in our political climate a theoretical game of economic science, far remote from practice and politics. For the time being, it seems to be impossible to combine economy and ecology in a joint market system. It is also a deception to see salvation in modern management: the frequently pursued conversion of the traditional city administration into a city management organised along the lines of business management for the 'enterprise city' often leads to a reduction of democratic control. This harms the remainders of still existing civic pride and sense of community: if city inhabitants see themselves only as clients of a service administration, which has to serve their individual interests, and if the important core tasks of local authorities, which have been fought for since the reforms of Freiherr vom Stein, are going to be privatised, even the last basis for a politically legitimised participatory planning is lost and with it ultimately also the identification with the city as a commonwealth.

What, then, is to be done? The precondition for a reorientation of town planning and urban design is not only to understand intellectually but also to accept as a basis for work that in the course of the Second Modern Age the city will be profoundly transformed and that even city profiles, spaces and city landscapes that appear externally unaltered will undergo a radical change of meaning. Admittedly, it is an uncomfortable experience that many – and particularly the serious – problems still seem to be disguised in the familiar images of city and country, and that their transformation will be recognised in outline only when they are closer scrutinised, questioned and investigated.

In this situation, town planning and urban design have three options:

- To continue as formerly and to hope that the pressure of the problems and the new reality will transform the traditional understanding of planning from within, because the existing planning system is flexible enough to be able to adjust with old structures to the new tasks. This conservative approach has its basis in the extraordinarily strong drive to perseverance and self-preservation of the existing political and administrative systems.
- To aim for fundamental reform, involving the establishment of new political and administrative regional authorities, with the intention to carry out appropriately profound changes

primarily in municipal self-administration, but also in respect of districts, regional councils and ministries. At present, however, things seem not to be going so badly that an administrative reform of the required scale could be politically achieved.

- However, there is a third option: not to look for salvation in an old or a new administrative structure, but to confront with wakeful perception the uncertainty of the future development, to rise to the challenge of the uncertainty of the decisions to be taken and to be open to new approaches. This means looking to find partial answers to individual problems and hope that something new will arise from them. Such an attitude, however, can only be adopted if we have goals and visions which offer hope for positive change and to set the bearings of a direction.[138]

With such an attitude, new opportunities open up, to pursue, beyond the resigned defence of the status quo, new targets and tasks which will again have a social and political dimension and will lead to new and interesting fields of work.

Before sketching some new scopes of tasks of this nature, the question should first briefly be addressed whether, despite all the trends to globalisation, any such thing as a particularly European town planning culture can and should exist.

The European tradition of town planning has major roots on the one hand in the progressive left-wing reform movements for the improvement of living conditions of the working classes and on the other in the conservative approaches, for example of the Arts and Crafts or the Home Defence movements, which in principle in addition to the protection of historical monuments also include the protection of the cultural landscape. European town planning has always understood itself on both its left progressive and its right conservative wing as a counterweight to the society- and culture-destroying forces of unrestrained industrialisation. These lines of tradition of European urban planning continue today, for example, in publicly subsidised housing, in the protection of historical monuments and in the strong movements for the protection of landscape and for ecology. In view of a naïve belief in progress, these basic characteristics of European urban planning must be maintained and developed further as a particular contribution of Europe to the cultivation of the urbanisation of the world. This has got nothing to do with planning works of a restorative nature following the Berlin model, but rather with a basic political and cultural understanding, which is not tied to any particular form of city.

The contemporary discussion is still too much restricted to the form of the city: here the compact European city, there the dissolved American urban sprawl. I regard this discussion as being unfruitful, because it avoids the real problems. By contrast, a comparison of the political goals and the procedures of town planning could be productive. From the perspective of social policy, the US city must be a warning to us to prevent large-scale social and economic segregation and aesthetic devastation with all our resources.[139] With regard to procedures of town planning and urban design, the traditional authority-stamped European town planning, however, should adopt certain elements of US town planning, which in terms of its economic liberal provenance are oriented towards private enterprise initiatives. Here, at present, we have an unsatisfactory position. In reality, developer-driven urban development in Europe in the past few years has gained enormously in importance. The 'European' planning culture, however, rejects the 'developer milieu' as immoral and uncultivated. By contrast, the 'American' developer milieu hardly takes any notice of planners and architects even in Europe. Both face each other with their mutual fears of being affected and their obvious prejudices. They must be brought together and enter into an intensive dialogue, with the objective of creating from 'local authority planning' and 'enterprise town planning' a third way with the objective of a 'quality agreement' on the development of cities and regions in Europe. This third way as the establishment of a new tradition must also be accepted as a kind of charter of urban development at the European level: European town planning and urban design cultures – and not only US and Asiatic urban development models – can and should make a specific, self-confident contribution to the unstoppable urbanisation of the world. For this purpose, however, it is necessary to get away from the narrow national and provincial perspective and to see even German and European urban development in a global perspective. Only in such a perspective will we be able to develop internationally binding principles and rules which make it possible to restrain an ecologically and culturally destructive, purely economically driven competition between the cities.

What specific planning tasks would be particularly urgent? Perhaps the greatest professional and political challenge consists in the cultivation of 'urban development without the city', as Wolf-gang Christ vividly describes the *Zwischenstadt*.[140] At the same time, he highlights its critical characteristics in a particularly strik-ing and tangible way, and I will adopt his terms and put them together here somewhat differently: 'space remains on the rack' and 'parts of the city are disappearing into the network'. 'Autistic centres' in the 'vacuum of the transit space' lead to 'vacuums in the old centres'. 'Outside the Old City pure functionalism is dominant' without 'a claim to design', with a 'throwaway mental-ity' in a 'space without characteristics', while within the Old City stage sceneries are dominant as crumbling bearers of symbols of a city myth, which is collapsing under the excessive load of concen-trated sentimentality.

The cultivation of the spaces of the *Zwischenstadt* as mediator between the isolated individual elements and the historical city, the building-up of 'value structures' in urban and landscape design in a city environment which has hitherto been abandoned to eco-nomic forces alone, would be a valuable, a typically European task and would make at the same time a globally valuable contri-bution to the spatial restraint and cultivation of an unleashed economy. Everything hangs on the gradual production of a new European cultural urban landscape, very much as a creative con-tinuation of the tradition of the old movement of the protection of homeland and landscape. Building on this tradition, concept and image must be developed for a new cultural landscape with pro-gressive urbanisation.

No less challenging than the cultivation of the devastating spatial effect of a globally unrivalled economy is the creation of new types of living spaces for groups of the population which have been sidelined by the globalisation of the economy as economically 'of no value'.

The threatening loss of home as a living world experienced as linked to a place and experienced as a whole is particularly bad for those parts of the population who rely on such local living worlds, and these are not only – as formerly in the old industrial society – children and young people with their parents, but also the old and the ill, people handicapped in their mobility, but also all those people who do not belong to the organised world of gainful employment with its division of labour. If these people can at all count on being able to stay in their homes, they frequently have to be content with the large social housing estates of the post-war period. In these estates, the loss can be particularly clearly shown: designed and conceived as residential facilities for a blooming, at the time well-paid and fairly homogeneous industrial society of skilled workers and employees without unemployment and with a clearly formulated division of labour and a stable basis of well-being, these urban areas have now frequently developed into a concentration of comparatively low-priced residential properties for poor, socially and culturally diverse groups of the population without professional and social prospects. In the past few decades, these residential facilities have furthermore lost their small-scale infrastructure of pubs, cinemas and corner shops little by little. What has been left are amputated parts of the city whose poverty is admittedly so far not externally visible, but which form the social dynamite of tomorrow.

On the basis of the objectives of the workers movement and their struggle for humane living conditions, it is a particularly European task to develop this town planning inheritance once again into holistic living areas and to create new types of space for the development of a self-determined life under substantially restricted economic conditions. The task is to generate living areas, in which local economies, admittedly modest and small-scale but for that reason largely independent of globalisation, can be developed.

The city in the Second Modern Age will not be able to get round a cultivation of the spatial effects of the globalised economy and a repair of the socio-spatial side-effects of modernism, if the rich tradition of European urban development which has a history of more than a thousand years is not be given up.

In connection with the creation of new fields of living and a cultivation of the landscape of progressive urbanisation, there is the task of giving the historical city cores, as particular parts of the city which cannot be reproduced and are of the highest symbolic significance, new functions and not simply to abandon them to a retail trade in crisis.

The systems of large traffic routes with nodes such as the

railway stations, petrol stations, rest points, shopping centres and dispatch warehouses which dominate the perception of many areas of the *Zwischenstadt* with their cheap throwaway architecture, must ultimately also be taken up as a major task of design.

In the age of electronic, digitalised media, which show the world only on-screen and in an overmighty, only instrumentally conceived non-aesthetic reality, counter-worlds must be created which can be experienced and understood with the senses and emotions and deserve therefore long-term affection and care.

For reasons of the retention of the natural basis of life, urban development in Europe must in future make do with the already existing built fabric: we must not draw on any new, hitherto undeveloped land and new uses must predominantly find a place in the existing building stock. Both are possible, because many more of the old industrial and military areas are becoming redundant, than are needed for new development, and because all in all we are using the existing buildings inadequately.

What we need to do is fight for a political recognition of these tasks, to search for political, social and cultural alliances and overcome the resigned attitude of today. The repair tasks must, so to speak, be 'transcended' in order to reach the new political, cultural and social conceptions and goals for the city in the Second Modern Age which are not wildly utopian in nature but have developed in response to conditions and constraints of day-today political reality and potential.

> Being political means ... regarding changing and even with considerable efforts no longer reversible processes not as a threat, but as an opportunity to rethink the horizon of one's own thinking, one's own activity. What we need is the willingness of architects and town planners to develop from being service providers ... into being protagonists, designers of the social horizon (Peter Neitzke).[141]

Thomas Sieverts
Bonn, November 1997

Postscript to the third edition

On dealing with uncertainty in urban development

In the postscript to the second edition I attempted to place the *Zwischenstadt* in connection with globalisation theories, to sketch a European perspective of urban design and to mark out major fields of action for town planning.[142] The postscript ends with the call for the architect, urban designer and town planner to think and act politically.

In the present postscript, I would like to go into the question of what it could today mean for the craft of urban design to think and act politically, if one understands 'becoming political' not only as the essential background, drive and benchmark for a socially responsible planning but tries to develop it as an integral component of generative thinking itself. The old approaches from the 1960s and 1970s essentially pursued the goal of the political nature of town planning through active participation of people at the receiving end in the design process and through active appropriation of the city space. These approaches still apply in principle today although the hopes initially connected with participation were not fulfilled because in the participation of the citizens, usually not the weaker citizens in need of protection, but that of the strong and in any case privileged interests prevails.

The craft of urban design remains in these respects usually quite conventional, indeed sometimes it is grossly simplified to make it accessible to the layman. Design as a specific form of professionally shaped creative thinking, the intellectual and at the same time visual and graphic creation of information of new worlds usually got the short end.

One of the reasons for this may have been that urban design was played out in a well-defined conceptual framework which believed that it could rely on a dependable programmatic basis of defined requirements. In those times of 'becoming political' which shaped my generation, one was still reasonably confident that one could predict the development of the city and the requirements of people if one only researched and analysed enough. Urban design showed a tendency to a kind of 'derivative urban design', which attempted to derive every design stage from an analytical finding: the more extensive the analysis, the better the plan. The hope of certainty bred of analysis has fundamentally dissolved, and this dissolution has now been well justified in epistemology and the theory of cognition. Our present view of urban development is shaped by the concept of uncertainty.

The reasons for this can be broadly summarised with bullet points: the fact that in principle the development of highly complex systems cannot be forecast;[143] the fact that the relationship of wanted effects and undesired side-effects in the collaboration of various socio-technical systems cannot be foreseen; the increasing satiation of basic existential requirements which comes with prosperity, with the consequence of more liberal, not easily predictable investment possibilities of time and money.

For these main reasons, research cannot remove this type of uncertainty, because it belongs precisely to the insoluble paradoxes that, despite the ever greater permeation of society with complex research-based rational systems, the paramount uncertainty of forecasting the system as a whole does not remove. City research, nevertheless, remains necessary and indispensable: it too cannot remove the principal uncertainty, but it can to a certain degree contain it.

In this predicament of urban development, the 'becoming political' of urban design must be redefined. It is no longer primarily a matter of the analytic derivation of clear, definable needs and programmes but the disclosure and illustration of new social and cultural opportunities, of new and also politically attractive possibilities in the form of rooms for manoeuvre and ranges of design. The main question that arises with regard to the nature of political margins and ranges of design is: In whose interest should they be used? We might mention as a suitable political goal and benchmark of planning action 'social justice'. But what does that mean today? As already remarked, references to the 'will of the citizens' are not sufficient for an answer to this question, and social advantages, the 'for whose good' question must be more thoroughly thought through, because there are no longer simple alternatives and because each alternative has its own undesired side-effects. Consequently, a broad spectrum of socio-economic arrangements must be examined, in order to find in the field of principal uncertainty a design approach which seems to be sufficiently robust to correspond to different forms of social justification. Becoming political has become demanding.

The following observations and thoughts are based on the one hand on experiences of dealing with programmatic uncertainty, as I experienced it during my work for the International Building Exhibition Emscher Park, and on the other on my work with talented students. In the field of academic experiments in the university, it is possible for new design methods and approaches to be easily tested and illustrated. Consequently, I rely primarily on student projects, but always with an eye to practice.

In their design projects focusing on the *Zwischenstadt* students tested certain new methodical design approaches, which sought to react creatively to the altered political situation. Analyses are no longer carried out with standard models, but more experimentally on different levels of simultaneous examination and therefore acquire more the character of general explanations. The question about how to handle uncertainty comes to the centre stage of the interest of design, and the concept of uncertainty is generatively worked at in its spatial and temporal aspects. What is at stake is the interpretation of the shape of only weakly determined structures in the barely centralised field of the *Zwischenstadt* and with scenarios which showed how these structures can graphically be developed over time.[144] This approach is thoroughly close to practice, since for example for much of the newly created fallow land there is no determinable market demand and it is also an open question whether there ever will be one. In these cases, even in practice, very clear limits to the functional derivation and justification of planning become visible.

What is needed in this situation of uncertainty is first of all a more creative way of how to deal with contrasts which cannot be resolved. Although the development is uncertain, there is a demand for forward-looking action, as though there were a goal.

The system world of globalisation tends to arbitrarily

adjustable 'ready to go' structures (Ernst Bloch); however, what is needed for the living world is the creation of culturally and topographically rooted places. Generally because of ignorance of complex causal connections, politics frequently takes thoughtless decisions which will be binding on future generations; what is needed, however, is a maximum degree of openness.

The tentative answers of talented students to the situation in the design treatment of the *Zwischenstadt* can only be lightly characterised as follows: *design with images and image-like processes*. Here, the design approaches switch between the discovery of politically activating, strongly atmospheric images and the design of form-giving processes of an economic, cultural and political nature.

Designing with *form-giving frameworks, cores and nodes*, with the qualification of open fields of development. The treatment of uncertainty in this design approach is bounded with the help of relatively 'classical' urban design resources. Networks of public place are linked to 'oases' of stable form-giving cores and nodes – both together form public development fields.

Designing in the dimensions of nature and time. In this design approach, new experiences are involved which have only become self-evident to the present generation of students: getting to know technically superannuated industrial and military fallow land – which nature has taken over again in a very short time, and where it remains undecided whether one should ascribe them rather to the realm of technology or to that of nature – stimulates conceptions of new building structures for socio-cultural functions and also as rich biotopes and at the same time designing also their possible transformations over time – transformation simulations which can be played out with computer-aided design in a broad spectrum of illustrative alternatives.

These different approaches share a positive attitude to uncertainty, which is expressed in the active assumption of uncertainty as an open space for hope. Uncertainty is understood as 'a challenge', as an adventure of urban development, as a space which cannot be determined and fixed but can be shaped through the projection of an activating image and can be brought into a specific 'disposition': this space cannot be 'defined' functionally, but one can at least give it a positive 'mood' in order to conceive it as an open space of possibilities.

This involves the courage to provide temporary solutions, for a revisable attempt of a 'bricolage'[145] of step-by-step design decisions, without determining an overall conception. This involves furthermore the courage to design simple unfinished 'initial wholes', which over time can evolve into individually unforeseeable, but much more complex and sustained wholes – a design method, of the kind which Christopher Alexander has developed with Heijo Neis in *A New Theory of Urban Design*.[146]

Any of these more or less tentative design methods has a political dimension of its own, which shapes the nature of design. What they have in common is, however, the great significance of images, whether in the form of stimulating metaphors, seductive images or the 'depiction' of atmospheres yearned for. Images seem to be especially well suited to holding back uncertainty and to providing the basis for designing in uncertainty. Images enter into the position of the unavailable specific justification and of the still open functional definition.

There is, however, a basic problem with the new role of beautiful images in urban design which is intensified by the almost unlimited possibilities for the production and manipulation of images offered by the computer. Here, in a simple way, a deceptive order of a picture world can be generated which looks conclusive and may therefore easily be taken for reality itself and seems to secure against being affected by crises: the step towards a world of the promotion of goods and self-deception with political rhetoric is then no longer very far.

However, this constantly present danger does not drive the power of images out of the world. The temptation to build up an image world unconnected to hard, conflict-intense reality can only be resisted if one confronts the reality and intervenes directly with real life without intermediate images. Only in the incessant confrontation of image and reality can the aesthetic nature of images develop a political power which is not misleading.

The design of activating images – Karl Ganser once spoke of 'temptation by beauty' – is most clearly inflamed in the design treatment of fallow land without functional and economic demand, which had frequently remained unknown as formerly 'forbidden' sites of industry and had therefore become part of the 'blind spots' of the city. For that reason, they are particularly well suited to inventive image projection.

The designing of images, or more precisely of atmospheres, stimulates the fantasy and occupies the vacuum of imagination with a 'space of hope'. When implemented, open, richly atmospheric stages are created, which stimulate play with them, adopting them and taking possession of them as a precondition for further developments which may materialise in the right circumstances. This type of designing is closely related to scenography and it is promoted and simplified by the diverse possibilities of digital image creation and manipulation.

The wakeful and politically critical implementation of this kind of designing represents a very creative approach: 'form follows fiction' (with fiction in the Anglo-Saxon sense understood as creative fantasy). Images of this type can also be understood as political target corridors which can be filled in differently within broad limits; they replace the precise place-specific intervention and control mechanisms which are no longer viable.

From the design of activating images it is only a single step to the design of a 'film', of a history of imagined political, economic and cultural processes, from which city structures and design elements will emerge.[147] Such urban design presupposes conception and construction of a client, of a concrete thought-out occurrence in space over a relatively long period. This type of design therefore demands, in addition to the purely spatial fantasy and power of imagination, also political and social imagination and procedural invention. This means that this type of design is very obviously political in nature – because social processes of a cultural and economic nature also have to be designed and accommodated, in which different interests and power ratios, but also institutions and procedures such as contracts for quality agreements, must also be allowed for.

Here too the dangers are obvious: not only students, but also architects and planners have a tendency to make their clients ideally 'appropriate' and to create illusionary imaginations of politics and society. The only help here is a never relaxing and intensive reflection on the experience of reality. This being given, this approach can very much promote complex design thinking: an important step on the road to a politically conceived profession, which does not end its design with the delivery of the finished work but takes on further creative responsibility in accompanying the 'life' of the work.

Atmospheric images and form-creating processes do not in themselves lead to spatial arrangements and structures: here, the mutually supplementary approaches of 'networks and nodes' or 'design cores and open fields' come into play. Both design approaches are particularly suitable to designing at the scale of the urban region of the *Zwischenstadt*: with the networks and their nodes, the *Zwischenstadt* can be 'grasped and measured'. The network is not hierarchic, it can be topologically distorted and, as a highly indeterminate system, it can be charged in differently within broad limits. The different network qualities and 'node potentials' can be designed and functionally specialised in a flexible equilibrium adaptable to changes. The network is therefore rightly a striking and suitable modern metaphor for the contemporary city and contemporary policy in which consolidated blocks of power have been replaced by fluid and constantly newly interacting powers and weights.

Network and nodes can in design terms be treated as the framework of the *Zwischenstadt* in such way that it becomes legible for the user, perhaps by the specific sign-like structuring of the nodes as 'interchange points' and the differentiation of the network routes, depending in each case on topography and function. In the network, system world and living world correspond with each other at least in part either intermittently or by sectors: for example, the transport and energy belts with the experience and the adventure of the nodes.

Here too there are very obvious dangers: this design approach has a tendency to allow these living worlds which are in spatial terms necessarily integrated to disappear in the network and to give a unilateral weight to technical communication. This can easily disadvantage the needs of the majority of the non-motorised part of the society. However, the design approach can also be applied to the development of slowness and the protection of 'withdrawal', for example in the formation of an integrated road network for unmotorised 'slow traffic'.

The latter design approach is supplemented by the approach of using long-lasting, significant and stable 'design cores' as 'oases of great architecture' and open, relatively transitory areas of the city. This mode of design seeks a synthesis of cores of stable permanence and broad areas of predominant indeterminacy. Indeterminacy, in this context, does not, however, mean design neutrality, but an atmospherically coloured openness of development that is determined by rules and restricted by a degree of 'naturalness' or 'artificiality'. Here, the political character of urban design as 'target or development corridor' is particularly clearly apparent, a development corridor which is pre-shaped by quality agreements.[148] Designing with 'nature and time' is superimposed on the above-mentioned design approaches.

Specifically when designing industrial fallow land, overgrown by nature, this allows the practical experience that the old contrast between nature and culture, between landscape and city no longer exists and that the cycles of construction, through uses to fallow land and derelict sites are often reduced to no more than one to two generations. Such experiences lead to experiments in the development of building areas which are at the same time high-quality biotopes, in which the landscape is built and the built fabric has a share of landscape qualities – as a continuum of technically monitored natural elements up to areas which are predominantly left 'free' to nature. The old contrast of technology and nature is 'suspended' in the third environment, which has both qualities.

The experience with urban fallow land and thinking in different natural shares of a built city world leads automatically to thinking in temporal changes in the form of temporal pauses and cycles. These theoretical concepts comprise thinking in cultural and economic utilisation cycles as much as in the dimensions of a development ecology, in which even through development new ecological opportunities for diversity of species are created. The dichotomy of 'bad building' and 'good nature' on which legislation is still based shows the tendency of being suspended as a step in the direction of a symbiotic city.

The design results generated by these lines of thought are too preliminary for it to be possible to assess them. However, they are politically creative to the extent that they sketch a new, fundamental way out of the dead end of existing intervention-compensation thinking, which is still based on an insuperable contrast between development and nature.[149]

The design approaches proposed here are already beginning to leave the academic area of the university: for example, in the design of fallow land in the Ruhr district, in considerations about the Rhine–Main Regional Park and in preliminary work for the

International Building Exhibition Prince Pückler Land in the Lausitz. When put together and superimposed, this type of urban design can be used for a policy which takes seriously the principal indeterminacy of urban development, which remains friendly to error and open to revision and which shows new routes to sustainability.

The openness of such urban design is, however, also its weakness: the design approaches are frequently removed from hard social reality. They oppose legal arrangements and regulations, procedures to be delegated and the possibility of technical calculation. They also demand other forms of participation in the direction of citizens' workshops, which deal not only with day-to-day conflicts but also with long-term issues. Consequently, planners and urban designers must at the same time work on the further development of the 'hard' tools in order to adjust them to the changed reality.

These design approaches are, however, in line with the current situation of urban development, in which the field of action of town planning can no longer be completely defined as a task prescribed 'externally' but as one in which the urban designers must rather contribute to formulating the tasks themselves in order to be able to discharge them in society. This requires – once again to repeat it for the last time – the 'parallel action' of active involvement in the politics of the city and also the professional further development of new urban design methods and their tools for implementation.

Thomas Sieverts
Bonn, March 1999

Notes

1 'The concepts of the dissolution of the compact city have a longer history of ideas'. In *Tomorrow: A Peaceful Path to Real Reform* (London, 1898). Later published as *Garden Cities of Tomorrow*, Ebenezer Howard had already regarded the 'small garden city' as a 'working model'. It would be followed, after experience had been collected, by 'a cluster of garden cities' in order finally to carry out 'a complete reconstruction of London'.

   Bruno Taut sketches with expressionistic pathos the 'dismantling of the stone city' and writes in the sketch: 'Let them collapse, the horrid constructions . . .', so that in floral forms of settlements visions of a new symbiosis of man and nature, built structure and landscape can be designed (in Bruno Taut, *Die Auflösung der Städte oder Die Erde eine gute Wohnung* [The Dissolution of the Cities or the Earth, a Good Home], Hagen, 1920, p. 1).

   From the criticism of the large city in the nineteenth century, through the garden city and life reform movement, through the manifestos and programmes for the new start in 1919, various paths lead to the concept of the 'urban landscape', which was formulated around 1940 and becomes the guiding principle for the reconstruction after 1945. Generations of planners yearned to dissolve the 'urban settlement mass' which was to be 'segmented and dispersed' in order to grow together with the landscape. At the start of the 1970s (heritage year 1975), the return of the yearning for the Old City becomes the counter-movement for the next generation against comprehensive redevelopment and the Modern Movement. (On this in detail, see Durth and Gutschow: *Träume in Trümmern: Stadtplanung 1940–1950* [Dreams in the Dust: Urban Planning 1940–1950], paperback edition, 1993, p. 214, chapter: Leitbilder für Stadtplanung [Guidelines for town planning].

2 See Martin Warnke, 'Natur nach dem Fall der Mauern' [Nature after the fall of the walls], quotation from Goethe's 'Wahlverwandtschaften' [Elective Affinities] (1807) (in *Dialektik* 2/1994, Zur Ästhetik des Territoriums [On the aesthetic of the territory].

3 See Rainer Mackensen: 'Ist Stadtentwicklung planbar?' [Can urban development be planned?], lecture on the retirement of Reinhart Breit, Technical University of Berlin, 1996 (unpublished lecture manuscript). Andreas Kagermeier: 'Jenseits von Suburbia – Tendenzen der Stadtentwicklung in der Region München aus verkehrsgeographischer Sicht' [Beyond suburbia – trends in the evolution of settlements in the region of Munich from the perspective of traffic geography] (in *Mitteilungen der Geographischen Gesellschaft in München* [Proceedings of the Geographical Society in Munich], 97th volume, Munich, 1994, edited by Reinhard Poesler and Konrad Rögner). Bundesforschungsanstalt für Landeskunde und Raumforschung [Federal Research Studies and Planning Research Institute], *Nachhaltige Stadtentwicklung: Herausforderung an einen resourcenschonenden und umweltverträglichen Städtebau* [Sustainable Urban Development: A Challenge to Resource Conservation and Environment-friendly Town Planning], Bonn-Bad Godesberg, February 1996).

4 See Robert Fishman, *Bourgeois Utopias: The Rise and Fall of Suburbia* (Basic Books, New York 1987); Robert Fishman, 'Die befreite Metropolis: Amerikas Neue Stadt' [The liberated metropolis: America's new city] (*Arch + Heft 109/110*, December 1991); Witold Rybczynski, *City Life: Urban Expectations in a New World* (Scribner, New York, 1995); Richard Louw, *America II: The Book that Captures Americans in Creating the Future* (Penguin Books, New York, 1985).

5 Examples of contemporary plans for major city expansions in Germany and Austria can be found in Klaus Gudzent and Thomas Sieverts, '*Platz für neue Wohnungen, städtebauliche Herausforderungen bei Stadterweiterungen der Zukunft*' [Place for new homes: town planning challenges in city expansions of the future] (*Information Forum for Town Planning Development Measures in North Rhine Westphalia*, Düsseldorf 1995). Also DISP, July 1995, pp. 43–52.

6 Olof Wärneryd, *Urban Corridors in an Urbanized Archipelago* (University of Lund, Lund, 1995).

7 See Eckard Ribbeck, 'Von der Peripherie zum Zentrum? – Verstädterung in Asien, Afrika, Lateinamerika' [From the periphery to the centre? – Urbanisation in Asia, Africa and Latin America] (*Deutsches Architktenblatt* DAB 12/95, p. 2330). Jürgen Oesterreich, *Elendsquartiere und Wachstumspole* [Slums and Growth Centres] (Deutscher Gemeindeverlag and Kohlhammer Verlag, Cologne and Stuttgart, 1980; especially p. 95: Überleben in ökonomischen Nischen [Survival in economic niches], Section: Hoher Grad der Raumnutzung [High degree of space utilisation].

8 Ministerium für Stadtentwicklung, Kultur und Sport des Landes Nordrhein-Westfalen [The Ministry of Urban Development, Culture and Sports of the Land of North Rhine Westphalia], *Memorandum II zu Inhalt und Organisation der Internationalen Bauausstellung*

Emscher Park [Memorandum II on the Content and Organisation of the International Building Exhibition Emscher Park, p. 9 (Düsseldorf, 1995).

9 Kurt Tucholsky wrote the poem 'The Ideal' in 1927. The first verse goes as follows:

> 'That's what you want, isn't it?:
> A villa in the countryside with a large terrace;
> at the front the Baltic Sea, at the back Friedrichstraße [Berlin's main street];
> with a beautiful view of mondaine countryside,
> from the bathroom you can see the Alps –
> but in the evening you don't have far to the cinema.
> The whole thing simple and modest.'

See Peter G. Rowe, *Making a Middle Landscape* (MIT Press, Cambridge, MA, 1991). Klaus Humpert, Sibylle Becker and Klaus Brenner, 'Entwicklung großstädtischer Agglomerationen' [Development of urban agglomerations]. In *Prozeß und Form 'natürlicher Konstruktionen'* [Process and forms of 'natural constructions'], edited by Klaus Teichmann and Joachim Wilke, Ernst und Sohn, Berlin, 1996, p. 182).

10 See Frank Lloyd Wright, *When Democracy Builds* (University of Chicago Press, Chicago, 1945). Gerd de Bruyn, *Die Diktatur der Philantropen* [The Dictatorship of Philanthropists] (Bauweltfundamente, Vieweg-Verlag, 1996). Ludwig Hilberseimer, *Entfaltung einer Planungsidee* [The Development of a Planning Idea] (Bauweltfundamente, Berlin, Frankfurt, Vienna, 1963).

11 See Pierre Frankenhauser, 'Fraktales Stadtwachstum' [Fractal city growth] (*Arch + Heft* 109/110, December 1991). Klaus Humpert, Sibylle Becker and Klaus Brenner, 'Entwicklung großstädtischer Agglomerationen' (see note 9).

12 See Mackensen (note 3).

13 See Ribbeck (note 7).

14 See Rainer Leppenies, 'Das Ende der Überheblichkeit' [The end of presumption] (in *Die Zeit* 48, 24 November 1995, p. 62).

15 See, for example, Andreas Feldkeller, *Die zweckentfremdete Stadt: Wider die Zerstörung des öffentlichen Raums* [The City Alienated from its Purpose: Against the Destruction of Public Space] (Frankfurt and New York, 1995). Dieter Hoftmann-Axthelm, *Die dritte Stadt* [The Third City] (Suhrkamp, Frankfurt, 1995). Fritz Neumeyer, 'Im Zauberland der Peripherie: Das Verschwinden der Stadt in der Landschaft' [In the enchanted land of the periphery: the disappearance of the city into the landscape] (in *Die verstädterte Landschaft* [The Urbanised Landscape], p. 31, edited by the Westphalia Arts Association, Münster, Aries Verlag, Munich, 1995). Günther Moeves, 'Die Stadt, die Arbeit und die Entropie' [The city, work and entropy] (*Jahrbuch für Architektur*, pp. 29–45, Frankfurt,

1995). Henning Kahmann, 'Was geändert werden muß, damit sich wirklich etwas ändert' [What has to be changed to achieve any real change] (Technical University Brunswick, Institute for Urban and Landscape Planning, unpublished manuscript). Andreas Brandt and Rudolf Böttcher, *Bauten und Projekte* [Buildings and projects] (Ernst und Sohn, Berlin, 1995), especially p. 46: Projekt für eine Stadt mit 200.000 Einwohnern in Karow und Brandenburg bei Berlin [Project for a city with 200,000 inhabitants in Karow and Blankenburg near Berlin].

16 Planning study for the city of Bonn by Thomas Sieverts.

17 The quasi-privatisation of the Zeil (the main shopping street in Frankfurt am Main) has been the subject for public discussion for a long time: since a competition in 1970, the roofing over of the Zeil has been discussed in order to give it the character of a shopping centre; the proposal was most recently brought up for discussion in 1994 (see *Frankfurter Rundschau* 30 November1994). The association of retailers of the Zeil, 'Zeil aktiv', demands that the Zeil be kept free of conspicuous drinkers, beggars and tramps as is usually the rule in shopping centres organised under private law. The city is meeting these demands through a surveillance service which seizes and removes conspicuous subjects and expects active collaboration and financial contribution by the retailers (see *Frankfurter Rundschau* of 14 and 15 June 1996 and *Frankfurter Allgemeine Zeitung* of 20 May 1995).

18 See The Magistrate of the City of Kassel, Director of Planning and Construction Uli Hellweg, *How Does One Build a City? Routes to the Unterneustadt* (Kassel, 1994).

19 See Rem Koolhaas, Generic Cities (in *S, M, L, XL, OMA* with Bruce Man, 010 Publishers, Rotterdam, 1995).

20 The discussion of urbanity was triggered by the lecture 'Urbanity' by Edgar Salin at the 11th general meeting of the Deutscher Städtetag [German city conference] in Augsburg, 1–3 June 1961, published in *Erneuerung unserer Städte* [Renewal of our cities], edited by the Deutsche Städtetag (W. Kohlhammer Publishers, Stuttgart and Cologne 1960). Salin emphasises the social, cultural and political dimensions of urbanity. The concept becomes fashionable, is turned into a technical concept, and ten years later Salin protests against its improper use as slogan: 'Urbanity is dead, and it is simply a lie to think that it could be resurrected, if the age of the masses lasts and if the masses are provided for with the corresponding tower blocks and traffic routes . . . Urbanity is a *form of life* which today cannot prosper anywhere' (E. Salin: Von der Urbanität zur 'Urbanistik' [From urbanity to 'urbanism'] (in *Kyklos*, vol. 23, 1970). After 'Urbanism through density' follows 'Urbanism as game of roles' in urban interaction (on the criticism, see Werner Durth, *Die Inszenierung der Alltagswelt* [The Staging of Day-to-Day Life], Brunswick and Wiesbaden, 1977). On trends of the 1980s, see H. Häußermann and W. Siebel, *Neue Urbanität* [New Urbanity]

(Frankfurt am Main, 1987). See also: Richard Sennett, *Rise and Fall of Public Man*.

21 See Susanne Hauser, *Urbane Wahrnehmungsformen: vom Über-leben alter Muster* [Urban Forms of Perception: On the Survival of Old Patterns], especially Chapter 3: Inszenierung alter Muster und neue Einkaufslust [Staging old patterns and the new love of shopping] (in *Stadt und Mensch zwischen Chaos und Ordnung* [City and man between chaos and order], edited by Dirk Roller, Peter Lang Publishers, Frankfurt am Main, 1996).

22 *Das Elbschwanenbüchlein* [the booklet on the River Elbe swans]. In memory of Johann Rist, imperial Count Palatine at Wedel, born 8th March 1607, died 31st August 1667. With extracts from his writings, by Albert Rode (Hamburg, 1907).

23 See Werner Durth, *Die Inszenierung der Alltagswelt, zur Kritik der Stadtgestaltung* [The staging of day-to-day life, on the critique of city design] (Brunswick, 1977). See Susanne Hauser, Note 21.

24 See *Der öffentliche Raum als Bühne* [The Public Space as Stage] (Friedrich Ebert Foundation, Bonn, 1994).

25 See H. Häußermann and W. Siebel, 'Die Festivalisierung der Politik und die Unsichtbarkeit der Städte' [The festivalisation of politics and the invisibility of the cities] (in Arno Brandt *et al.*, *Das Expo-Projekt, Weltausstellung und die Stadt der Zukunft* [The Expo Project, World Exhibition and the City of the Future], Hannover, 1991). See Thomas Sieverts, 'Städtebau im Zeichen städtischen Nutzungswandels – Perspektiven für den öffentlichen Raum' [Town planning in times of changing urban use patterns – prospects for public space] (in *SIA Schweizer Ingenieur und Architekt*, 108th annual, November 1990). Thomas Sieverts, 'Die Gestaltung des öffentlichen Raums' [The design of public space] (in *Die Stadt – Ort der Gegensätze* [The city – place of contrasts], Demokratische Gemeinde (special edition), Bonn, March 1996).

26 On the socio-economic and socio-cultural 'System Tokyo', see Michael Wegener, *Urban Planning in Tokyo: a European perspective* (University of Dortmund, no date).

27 See Christopher Alexander, 'A city is not a tree' (in *Architectural Forum*, New York, April/May 1965, pp. 58–62).

28 See Günther Moewes, 'Die Stadt, die Arbeit und die Entropie' [The city, employment and entropy] (*Jahrbuch für Architektur*, Frankfurt, 1995).

29 See Ullrich Hatzfeld and Stefan Kruse, 'Reale Planung in Traum-welten – Freizeitgroßanlagen als wachsendes Planungsproblem' [Real planning in dream worlds – large-scale leisure facilities as a growing planning problem] (in *PlanerIn, SRL-Mitteilungen* 3/95, p. 22).

30 See Imke Bonin, *Wohn-Dichte Zwei Komma Null* [Residential Density Two Point Zero] (Series of papers by the Department of Architecture vol. 22, University of Kassel, Kassel, 1995).

31 See Jane Jacobs, *The Death and Life of Great American Cities*

(Random House, New York, 1961); German edition, *Bauweltfundamente* vol. 4, 4th edition 1993).

32 See Empirica (Jürgen Aring, Ulrich Pfeiffer, Andrea Opitz and Bernhard Faller), *Von der Regionalplanung zur regionalen Entwicklungsplanung* [From Regional Planning to Regional Development Planning] (experts' report, Bonn, November 1995).

33 See Thomas Sieverts, 'Von der parasitären zur symbiotischen Stadt – zu einer neuen Charta des Städtebaus' [From the parasitic to the symbiotic city – on a new charter of urban planning] (in *Wohn-Stadt*, edited by Martin Wentz, pp. 29–33, Campus Verlag, Frankfurt, 1993).

34 See Katharina Feldhusen, Daniel Gut and Christian Moczalla, *Nulloptionen: Stadtplanung ohne Bauen, am Beispiel der Wohnungssituation in Frankfurt* [Zero Option: Town Planning without Construction, Using the Example of the Residential Situation in Frankfurt] (Department of Architecture, Technical University of Darmstadt, 1990). Detlev Ipsen, 'Das Überleben der Städte: Ökologische Perspektiven der Lebensqualität' [The survival of cities: ecological prospects for the quality of life] (in *Universitas*, January 1996).

35 See Ribbeck, note 7.

36 See Dieter Hoffmann-Axthelm, *Die dritte Stadt* [The Third City] (Suhrkamp Publishers, Frankfurt ,1995).

37 See Ludovica Scarpa, *Gemeinwohl und lokale Macht, Honoratioren und Armenwesen in der Berliner Luisenstadt im 19. Jahrhundert* [Social Well-Being and Local Power, Local Dignitaries and Charity Systems in the Luisa Suburb of Berlin in the Nineteenth Century]. Quotation from Hobrecht on social mixture, pp. 233 ff. (Munich and Paris, 1995).

38 See Jane Jacobs, note 31.

39 See Hatzfeld and Kruse, note 29.

40 See William A. Mitchell, *City of Bits: Space, Place and the Infobahn*, p. 46, Recombinant Architecture (MIT Press, Cambridge, MA, 1995).

41 See Daniel Cohn-Bendit and Frank Herterich, 'Differenz und Kommune' [Difference and commune] (in *Planungskulturen* [Planning cultures], edited by Martin Wentz, Campus Verlag, Frankfurt, 1992). Frank Herterich, 'Planung für eine multikulturelle Stadt?' [Planning for a multicultural city?] (in *Risiko Stadt?: Perspektiven der Urbanität* [Risk City?, Prospects for Urbanity], edited by Ullrich Schwarz, with the collaboration of Dirk Meyhöfer, p. 193 (Hamburg, 1994). The basic data for both approaches were from 1987, more recent data of about 1993 can be found in the new edition of the *Frankfurter Socialatlas* [Social Atlas of the City of Frankfurt].

42 See Karl Ganser, 'The ecologically, economically and socially compatible city – a utopia?' (Lecture at the 'Building Forum' in Münster, Westphalia, February 1996, publication planned).

43 See Thomas Sieverts, note 33.

44 See Thomas Sieverts, 'Neue Aufgaben für den Städtebau im alten Europa – Voraussetzungen, Prinzipien, Beispiele' [New tasks for town planning in old Europe – conditions, principles and examples] (in *Zukunftsaufgaben der Stadtplanung* [Future Tasks for Town Planning], edited by T. Sieverts, Werner Verlag, Düsseldorf, 1990).

45 See Herbert Sukopp (ed.), *Stadtökonomie: das Beispiel Berlin* [City Ecology: the Example of Berlin] (Dietrich Renner Verlag, Berlin, 1990). Dirk Maxeiner and Michael Miersch, 'Im Dickicht der Städte' [In the thicket of cities] (in *Die Zeit* 18, 26th April 1996).

46 See Susanne Hauser, 'Repräsentationen der Natur- und Umweltmodelle' [Representation of natural and environmental models] (*Zeitschrift für Semiotik*, vol. 18, part 1, 1996).

47 See Klaus Neumann and Thomas Sieverts, *Das Meßdorfer Feld: Konzeptionelle Ansätze für eine langfristige und ökologisch orientierte Sicherung und Weiterentwicklung* [The Meßdorfer Field: Conceptual Approaches for its Long-Term and Ecologically Based Protection and Further Development] (planning experts' report for the City of Bonn, May 1995).

48 See Hansjörg Küster, *Geschichte der Landschaft in Mitteleuropa* [History of the Landscape in Central Europe] (C.H. Beck Verlag, Munich, 1995).

49 See Klaus Neumann, note 47.

50 Wilhelm Ripl and Christian Hildmann, 'Ökosysteme als thermodynamische Notwendigkeit' [Ecosystems and thermodynamic necessity] (in O. Fränzle, F. Müller and W. Schröder, *Handbuch der Umweltwissenschaften* [Manual of Environmental Science], Landsberg, 1997).

51 See Thomas Sieverts (ed.), *Perspektiven künftiger Siedlungsentwicklung* [Prospects for Future Settlement Development] (Technical University of Darmstadt papers on science and technology 50, Darmstadt, 1989).

52 See Martin Buchholz, 'Biofeedback – Aspekte einer nachhaltigen Stadtentwicklung' [Biofeedback – aspects of sustainable urban development] (unpublished manuscript, Technical University of Berlin, Institute of Landscape Architecture, Berlin, 1995).

53 See Thomas Sieverts, 'Chancen des alltäglichen Umbaus – Städtebauliche Aspekte der Recycling-Disskussion' [Opportunities for day-to-day conversions – town planning aspects of the recycling discussion] (in *Deutsches Architektenblatt* 8/1993, SW 241).

54 See Klaus Neumann, note 47.

55 See Karl Ganser, note 8.

56 Susanne Hauser, 'Garbage, waste and boundaries' (in Jeff Bernard *et al.* (eds) *Welt der Zeichen, Welt der Ding*, [World of Signs, World of Things], OGS, Vienna, 1977, pp. 73–86).

57 See Karl Ganser, 'Landschaftstypen im Emscher Raum: Zur Frage ihrer Schutzwürdigkeit' [Landscape types in the Emscher region: on the question whether they deserve preservation] (in *Natur und*

Landschaft, vol. 10/1995: *Naturschutz in der Industrielandschaft* [Nature preservation in the industrial landscape]).

58 See Kevin Lynch, *The Image of the City* (MIT Press, Cambridge, MA, 1960).

59 Alain Touraine, 'Die Stadt – Ein überholter Entwurf?' [The city – an outdated design?] (in *Die Stadt, Ort der Gegensätze* [The city, place of contrasts], special edition of *Demokratische Gemeinde*, the monthly magazine on local authority policy, Bonn, March 1996).

60 See André Gorz, *Kritik der ökonomischen Vernunft: Sinnfragen am Ende der Arbeitsgesellschaft* [Critique of Economic Reason: Essential Questions at the End of the Employment Society] (Rotbuch-Verlag, Berlin, 1989).

61 On the pluralisation of lifestyles, see Ulrich Beck, 'Jenseits von Stadt und Klasse?' [Beyond position and class?] (in Kreckel (ed.) *Soziale Ungleichheiten* [Social Inequities], Göttingen 1983). Ulrich Beck and Elisabeth Beck-Gernsheim (eds), *Riskante Freiheiten: Individual-isierung in modernen Gesellschaften* [Risky Freedoms: Individualisation in Modern Societies] (Frankfurt am Main, 1994). The concept of 'bricolage-biographies' is discussed by Ronald Hitzler in *Kleine Lebenswelten: Ein Beitrag zum Verstehen von Kultur* [Small Living Worlds: A Contribution to the Understanding of Culture] (Opladen, 1988).

62 See Richard Sennett, 'Etwas ist faul in der Stadt' [Something is rotten in the city] (*Die Zeit*, 5, 1996).

63 See Detlev Ipsen, 'Das Überleben der Städte: Ökologische Perspektiven der Lebensqualität' [The survival of cities: ecological perspectives on the quality of life] (*Universitas*, January 1996).

64 Evan McKenzie, University of Illinois/Chicago, quoted in Witold Rybczynski *City Life: Urban Expectations in a New World*, p. 182 (Scribner, New York, 1995).

65 See Gunnar Törnqvist, 'On arenas and systems' (in *Space and Time in Geography, Essays Dedicated to Torsten Hägerstrand*, University of Lund, Lund, 1981).

66 As the basic text on the history and philosophy of the separation of the sphere of employment and the sphere of (social) interaction, see Jürgen Habermas, 'System und Lebenswelt' [System and living world] (in *Theorie des kommunikativen Handelns* [Theory of Communicative Action]), vol. 2: *Zur Kritik der funktionalistischen Vernunft* ... [On the Critique of Functionalist Reason ...] (Suhrkamp, Frankfurt am Main, 1981). On the relationship between technical advance and social living world, see also the earlier works of Jürgen Habermas, such as *Technik und Wissenschaft als Ideologie* [Technology and science as ideology] (Frankfurt am Main, 1968).

67 See Marc Augé, *Orte und Nicht-Orte: Vorüberlegungen zu einer Ethnographie der Einsamkeit* [Places and Non-Places: Considerations on an Ethnography of Loneliness] (Fischer Verlag, Frankfurt am Main, 1996); Helge Drafz, 'Heimatlos und unterwegs: Vom

Ende des Regionalismus' [Homeless and on the move: on the end of regionalism] (in *Scheidewege*, vol. 25, 1995/6).

68 See Ullrich Hatzfeld, note 29.

69 See Torsten Hägerstrand, *What about People in Regional Science?* (Regional Science Association, Papers, vol. XXIV, 1970). Also 'Space, time and human condition' (in *Dynamic Allocation of Urban Space*, edited by A. Karlqvist, L. Lundqvist and F. Snickers, Sax House, Westmead, Hants, 1975). Also, 'Time-geography: focus on the corporeality of man, society and Environment, (in *The Science and Praxis of Complexity*, The United Nations University, Tokyo, 1985).

70 See Alan Touraine, note 59.

71 See Torsten Hägerstrand, note 69.

72 Tora Friber, *Everyday Life: Woman's Adaptive Strategies in Time and Space* (The Swedish Council for Building Research, Stockholm, 1993).

73 Göderitz, Rainer and Hoffmann, *Die gegliederte und aufgelockerte Stadt* [The Well-Ordered and Dispersed City] (Wasmuth Publishers, Tübingen, 1957).

74 Hartmut and Helga Zeiher, *Orte und Zeiten der Kinder* [Places and Times for Children] (Juventa-Verlag, Weinheim and Munich, 1994).

75 See Olof Wärneryd, *Urban Corridors in an Urbanized Archipelago* (University of Lund, Lund, 1995).

76 See Karl Ganser, note 42.

77 See Olof Wärneryd, note 75.

78 Hartmut Hässermann and Walter Siebel, *Soziologie des Wohnens. Eine Einführung im Wandel und Ausdifferenzierung des Wohnens* [Sociology of Dwelling: An Introduction to the Changes and Differentiation of Dwelling] (Juventus Verlag, Weinheim, 1996).

79 See I. I. T. M. Geerards, 'The spatial organization of integral chain management' (lecture manuscript, not published, without date). Thomas Sieverts and Karl Ganser: 'Vom Aufbaustab Speer zur Internationalen Bauausstellung und darüber hinaus' [From the development staff Speer to the International Building Exhibition and beyond (in *Bauplatz Zukunft: Dispute über die Entwicklung von Industrieregionen* [The building site for the future, disputes about the development of industrial regions], edited by Rolf Kreibich, Arno S. Schmid, Walter-Siebel, Thomas Sieverts and Peter Zlonicky, Klartext Verlag, Frankfurt am Main, 1994).

80 See Karl Ganser, note 42.

81 Walter Kahlenborn, Meinolf Dierkes, Camilla Krebs-Gnath, Sophie Mützel, Klaus W. Zimmermann, *Berlin: Zukunft aus eigener Kraft, ein Leitbild für den Wirtschaftsstandort Berlin* [Berlin: Future under its Own Steam, a Guiding Image for Berlin as Business Location] (FAB Publisher, Berlin, 1995).

82 On the interaction of culture, literature, advertising and land speculation see Mike Davis, *City of Quartz: Ausgrabungen der Zukunft*

in Los Angeles [Excavations of the Future in Los Angeles] (Berlin and Göttingen, 1994).

83 Fritz Neumeyer, 'Im Zauberland der Peripherie: Das Verschwinden der Stadt in der Landschaft' [In the wonderland of the periphery: the disappearance of the city into the landscape] (in *Die verstädterte Landschaft* [The Urbanised Landscape], edited by the Westphalian Arts Association Münster, Aries-Verlag, Munich, 1995).

84 W. I. Neutelings, 'Erkundung des Wunderlandes. Eine Fahrt durch die Peripherie der Niederlande' [The exploration of the wonderland. A journey through the periphery of the Netherlands] (in *Die verstädterte Landschaft* [The urbanised landscape], see note 83).

85 Pierluigi Nicolin, 'Notizen zu Peripherie – Metropole – Loslösung' [Notes on Periphery – Metropolis – Detachment] (in *archithese* 6/92, p. 57).

86 Quoted by Susanne Hauser in her paper, 'Abfall und Gestaltung: Zur Ästhetik aufgegebener Industrieareale' [Waste and design formation: on the aesthetic of abandoned industrial areas] (unpublished manuscript, Berlin, March 1996).

87 See Susanne Hauser, note 86.

88 Wolfgang Welsch, 'Zur Aktualität ästhetischen Denkens' [On the topicality of aesthetic thinking] (in *Ästhetisches Denken* [Aesthetic Thinking], Reclam-Verlag, Stuttgart, 3rd edition, 1993).

89 Wolfgang Welsch, 'Perspektiven für das Design der Zukunft' [Prospects for the design of the future] (in *Ästhetisches Denken* [Aesthetic Thinking], see note 88).

90 See Ulrich Beck, 'Die offene Stadt' [The open city] (in *Deutsches Architektenblatt* DAB, March 1996, pp. 362–365).

91 Key-word 'John Cage' (in *The New Grove Dictionary of Music and Musicians*, London, 1980, vol. 3, p. 601).

92 See Pasqual Amphoux, *Aux écoutes de la ville, la qualité sonore des espaces publiques européens: Méthode d'analyse comparative, enquête sur trois villes suisses* (with German summary), (Swiss National Fund for the promotion of Scientific Research, programme City and Traffic, 1995). Stimulating examples (with a CD-Rom) can be found in Isabelle Faust, Detlev Ipsen, Justin Winkler and Hans U. Werner (eds), *Klangwege* [Sound Paths] (University of Kassel, Kassel, 1995).

93 Frank Lloyd Wright, *When Democracy Builds* (University of Chicago Press, Chicago, 1945).

94 Works of Kevin Lynch, all MIT Press, Cambridge, MA, USA, *The Image of the City* (1960), *Site-Planning* (1962/71), *View from the Road* (with Appleyard and Myer, 1966), *What Time is this Place?* (1972), *Managing the Sense of a Region* (1976), *A Theory of Good City Form* (1981), *City-Sense and City-Design: Writings and Projects* (edited by T. Banerjee and M. Southworth, 1990).

95 Christopher Tunnard and Boris Pushkarev, *Man-Made America – Chaos or Control? An Inquiry into Selected Problems of Design in*

the Urbanized Landscape (Yale University Press, New Haven, CT, 1963).

96 Works of Christopher Alexander: *Notes on the Synthesis of Form* (Harvard University Press, Cambridge, MA, 1964); with Murray Silverstein, Schlomo Angel, Sarah Ishikawa and Denny Abrams, *The Oregon Experiment* (Oxford University Press, New York, 1975); *A Timeless Way of Building* (Oxford University Press, New York, 1979); with Sara Ishikawa and Murray Silverstein. *A Pattern Language* (Oxford University Press, New York, 1977); with Hajo Neis, Artemis Aminou and Ingrid King, *A New Theory of Urban Design* (Oxford University Press, New York, 1987).

97 Robert Venturi, Denise Scott-Brown and Steven Izenour, *Learning from Las Vegas* (MIT Press, Cambridge, MA, 1972).

98 Colin Rowe and Fred Koetter, *Collage City* (MIT Press, Cambridge, MA, 1978). Quotation by Bernhard Hoesli in the postscript to his translation 1984, p. 237).

99 Colin G. Rowe, *Making a Middle Landscape* (MIT Press, Cambridge, MA, 1991).

100 Peter Calthorpe, *The Next American Metropolis* (Princeton Architectural Press, New York, 1993).

101 Rem Koolhaas, *S, M, L, XL* (OMA, with Bruce Man, 010 Publishers, Rotterdam, 1995).

102 See Walter Kahlenborn, Meinolf Dierkes *et al.*, note 81.

103 See Gerhard Schneider, 'Kognitive Karten und Kartierungen: Orientierungsbezogene Umweltpräsentation' [Cognitive maps and mapping: Orientation related presentation of the environment] (in Kruse, Graumann and Lantermann (eds), *Ökologische Psychologie* [Ecological Psychology], Munich, 1990, p. 268).

104 See the entry on 'Perception' in the *Encyclopaedia Britannica* (Macropaedia).

105 See Stephan Willinger, 'Die narrative Stadtanalyse – Eine experimentelle Planungsmethode' [The narrative city analysis – an experimental planning method] (*Raumplanung*, vol. 71, December 1995).

106 Those interested can consult StadtReisen Berlin e.V. (Berlin and Potsdam on foot, city explorations), Malplaquetstr. 5, 13347 Berlin-Wedding).

107 See Amos Rapaport and R. Kantor, 'Komplexität und Ambivalenz in der Umweltgestaltung' [Complexity and ambiguity in environmental design] (*AIP-Journal* July 1967).

108 See entry on 'Musikpsychologie' (music psychology) in the chapter 'Gehör' (hearing) (in *MGG, die Musik in Geschichte und Gegenwart* [Music in history and the present time], Bärenreiter and Metzler-Verlag, 1995) and entry on 'Gedächtnis' [memory] (in *Riemann Musik-Lexikon*, p. 319).

109 See the entry on 'Perception', note 104.

110 Jahrhunderthalle [millennium hall] Bochum.

111 André Heller: Theme Park draft currently in preparation, not yet published.

112 Duisburg-Meiderich. See Martin Linne, 'Vom Konzept zur Real-isierung – Landschaftspark Duisburg-Nord' [From conception to realisation – Landscape Park Duisburg North] (in *Garten + Land-schaft*, 7, 1994, pp. 20–24).

113 The Gasometer in Oberhausen. See Ulrich Borsdorf (ed.), *Feuer und Flamme: 200 Jahre Ruhrgebiet* [Fire and Flame: 200 Years of the Ruhr District]. Essen: Klartext-Verlag, 1994.

114 'Ich Phoenix' [I Phoenix']. An artistic event with contributions by Ongo Bartsch, Christoph Blase, Karl Ganser, Kai-Uwe Hemken, Uwe Rüth and Rolf Wedewer. Essen: Klartext-Verlag, 1996.

115 Mechtenberg Floral Festival. See Kommunalverband Ruhrgebiet [The Regional Council of the Ruhr District] (ed.): *Der Land-schaftspark Mechtenberg: Ein Modellprojekt des Kommunalverban-des Ruhrgebiet im Rahmen des Internationalen Bauausstellung Emscher Park* [The Landscape Park Mechtenberg: A Model Project of the Regional Council of the Ruhr District in the Context of the International Building Exhibition Emscher Park], Essen, 1994.

116 'Aufbrechen Amerika' [Setting out for America], music festival in North Rhine Westphalia 1992/93, organised by the City of Bochum and the Bochum Symphony Orchestra in collaboration with the Ministry of Culture of North Rhine Westphalia. The catalogue, Bochum 1992.

117 The Schurenbach Heap, an artificial mountain of colliery waste. See Triennale Ruhr GmbH (ed.), 'Landmarken – Zeichen des Wandels' [Landmarks – signs of change], unpublished manuscript.

118 Bottrop – Viewing steel pyramid. See 'Der Halde die Krone augesetzt' [crowning the waste heap], in *Emscher Park Informatio-nen*, 45, 11/1995, pp. 1–3, edited by the International Building Exhibition Emscher Park.

119 Federal Garden Festival Nordstern. See Bundesgartenschau 1997 Gelsenkirchen GmbH (ed.), *BUGA 97*, Gelsenkirchen, 1995.

120 Riphorst Wood Garden. See IBA [International Building Exhibition] Emscher Park (ed.), *Projekte des IBA Emscher Park in Oberhausen* [Projects of the IBA Emscher Park in Oberhausen], Gelsenkirchen, 1996.

121 See Proposals of the Association of Planning Authorities for the amendment of the Federal statute-book (c/o Bund Deutscher Architekten [Association of German Architects], Bonn, May 1995).

122 See Thomas Sieverts: 'Art and architecture: "nice addition, compre-hensive work of art or something else" and the response by Gert Selle: Art – the salt in the soup of planning, as a comprehensive work of art?' (in *Bauplatz Zukunft – Dispute über die Entwicklung von Industrieregionen* [The Building Site Future – Disputes about the Development of Industrial Regions], see note 79).

123 See Karl Ganser, note 8.

124 See Kevin Lynch, *Managing the Sense of the Region* (Cambridge, MA, 1976).

125 See Thomas Sieverts and Karl Ganser: 'Vom Aufbaustab Speer zur

Internationalen Bauausstellung Emscher Park und darüber hinaus' [From the design staff Speer to the International Building Exhibition and beyond] (see note 79).

126 Hanns Adrian, 'Stadt und Region, Konzentration oder Dekonzentration?' [City and region, concentration or diffusion?] In Informationszentrum Beton (ed.), *Stadtstrukturen: Status quo und Modelle für die Zukunft* [City Structures. Status Quo and Models for the Future] (Düsseldorf, 1997).

127 See Peter Calthorpe, *The Next American Metropolis* (Princeton Architectural Press, New York, 1993).

128 See Hanns Adrian, note 126.

129 This categorical imperative is formulated by Christian Morgenstern in his poem 'Die unmögliche Tatsache' [The impossible fact], published in Zurich in 1981 under the title 'Alte Galgenlieder' [Old gallow songs]. The poem tells the story of an elderly gentleman named Palmström who gets run over by a car on a street corner. His attempt to explore how this could have come about leads him to the conclusion that the accident could not have happen because the car was not allowed to drive in the street. Here is a rough translation of the last two verses of the poem:

> Wrapped in damp cloths
> he studies the statute books
> and establishes soon clarity:
> cars were not allowed to drive there.
> And he comes to the resolution
> that the experience was but a dream
> because, so his razor sharp conclusion,
> what shall not be, cannot be.

130 Heiner Müller quotes Eckhard Siepmann (Werkbundarchive, Berlin, 1996).

131 J. Pietsch, 'Stadt Landschaften – neue Wahrnehmungsformen für Ballungsräume' [City landscapes – new forms of perception for urban regions] (unpublished manuscript, Institute for Urban Ecology at the Technical University of Hamburg-Harburg, April 1996).

132 Ulrich Beck, *Risikogesellschaft* [The Risk Society], Suhrkamp, Frankfurt, 1986; Anthony Giddens, *Jenseits von Links und Rechts: Die Zukunft radikaler Demokratie* [Beyond Left and Right: The Future of Radical Democracy], Suhrkamp, Frankfurt, 1996; Ulrich Beck, Anthony Giddens and Scott Lash, *Reflektive Modernisierung, Eine Kontroverse* [Reflexive Modernisation: A Controversy], Suhrkamp, Frankfurt, 1996.

133 See Klaus Neumann, Thomas Sieverts, 'Vom bösen Bauen und der guten Natur' [On evil construction and good nature], in *DISP Dokumente and Informationen Schweizer Planer* [Documents and Information of Swiss Planners], vol. 128, January 1997.

134 See Anthony Giddens, 'Leben in einer posttraditionalen Gesellschaft'

[Life in a post-traditional society], in Beck *et al.* op. cit., pp. 113–194.

135 See Ulrich Beck (ed.), *Kinder der Freiheit* [Children of Freedom], Suhrkamp, Frankfurt, 1996.

136 See note 1.

137 See Marc Augé, *Orte und Nicht-Orte: Vorüberlegungen zu einer Ethnologie der Einsamkeit* [Places and Non-places: Considerations on an Ethnology of Loneliness], Frankfurt am Main, 1994.

138 See Thomas Sieverts, Karl Ganser, 'Vom Aufbaustab Speer zur Internationalen Bauausstellung Emscher Park und darüber hinaus' [From the development staff Speer to the International Building Exhibition and beyond], in *Bauplatz Zukunft: Dispute über die Entwicklung von Industrieregionen* [The Building Site of the Future: Disputes about the Development of Industrial Regions], edited by Rolf Kreibich, Arno S. Schmid Walter-Siebel, Thomas Sieverts and Peter Zlonicky, Klartext Publishers, Frankfurt/Main, 1994.

139 See Peter Neitzke, Carl Steckeweh and Reinhard Wustlich (eds), *CENTRUM: Jahrbuch Architektur und Stadt* [Annual of Architecture and City] *1997–1998*, chapter 'Exit Downtown', Vieweg, Wiesbaden, 1997.

140 See Wolfgang Christ, 'Wertstrukturen in der Stadtplanung' [Value structures in town planning], in *Deutsches Architektenblatt* [German Architects Journal] 9/97, pp. 1244–1245.

141 See Peter Neitzke, 'Nachfrage: Wann werden Architekten politisch?' [The question is: when will architects become political?], in *Baumeister*, October 1997.

142 See Thomas Sieverts, 'Die Stadt in der Zweiten Moderne: Eine europäische Perspektive' [The city in the Second Modern Age, a European perspective]. In Bundesamt für Bauwesen und Raumordnung [Federal Office of Construction and Spatial Allocation] (ed.), *Informationen zur Raumplanung* [Information on Spatial Planning)], vol. 7/8 1998, pp. 455–473.

143 See Gerhard Gamm: *Flucht aus der Kategorie: Positivierung des Unbestimmten als Ausgang aus der Moderne* [Flight from the Category: A Positive View of the Indeterminate as a way out of the Modern], Suhrkamp, Frankfurt am Main, 1994. Gerhard Gamm, 'Anthropomorphia inversa: Über die Medialisierung von Mensch und Technik' [On man and technology: the age of electronic media]. In *Lettre International 89*, summer 1998.

144 See Joachim Schöffel and Thomas Sieverts (eds). Zukunft Rhein-Main: Die Gestaltung einer regionalen Lebenswelt [The future of the Rhine-Main: the forming of a regional living world], in *Forschung und Entwurf in Städtebau und Architektur* [Research and Design in Urban Design and Architecture] 4/1999); Wilhelm, Wiegand and Sieverts (eds), *Städtebau im Zeitalter der Globalisierung* [Urban Development in the Age of Globalisation] and *Das Transatlantische Entwurfsstudio USA 4* (Forschung und Entwurf in Städtebau und Architektur [The Transatlantic Design Studio USA 4 (Research and

Design in Urban Design and Architecture 5/1999)]. Both publications: Department of architecture, Technical University of Darmstadt, El Lissitzky Strasse 1, 64287 Darmstadt.

145 See Wolfgang Christ, 'Zur Gestalt and Gestaltung künftiger Siedlungsräume: Bricolage statt Plan Voisin' [On the shape and design of future settlements spaces. Bricolage instead of Plan Voisin]. In Bundesamt für Bauwesen und Raumordnung (ed.), *Stadt-Landschaft* [City Landscape] (Information on Spatial Development, vol. 7/8 1998), pp. 475–482.

146 Christopher Alexander, Hajo Neis, Artemis Aminou and Ingrid King: *A New Theory of Urban Design*, Oxford University Press, New York, 1987.

147 See Thomas Sieverts: Bild und Berechnung im Städtebau [Image and calculation in urban design]. In *Information und Imagination*, Munich, 1973.

148 See Wolfgang Christ (see note 145).

149 See Klaus Neumann and Thomas Sieverts: Vom bösen Bauen und der guten Natur [On bad building and good nature]. In *DISP Dokumente und Information zur schweizerischen Orts-, Regional- und Landesplanung* [Documents and Information for Swiss Local, Regional and State Planning], ORL Institute, Zurich, vol. 128, January 1997.

Index

Page references for illustrations are in *italics*; those for notes are followed by n